MIDDLE EASTERN

MIDDLE EASTERN

VIBRANT, FLAVORFUL
EVERYDAY RECIPES

Project Editor Siobhán O'Connor
Project Designer Alison Shackleton
Editor Kiron Gill
US Editors Nathalie Mornu, Lori Hand
US Consultant Renee Wilmeth
Jacket Designer Alison Donovan
Jackets Coordinator Jasmin Lennie
Production Editor David Almond
Senior Producer Luca Bazzoli
Managing Editor Dawn Henderson
Managing Art Editor Alison Donovan
Art Director Maxine Pedliham
Publishing Director Katie Cowan

First American Edition, 2022
Published in the United States by DK Publishing
1450 Broadway, Suite 801, New York, NY 10018

Copyright © 2022 Dorling Kindersley Limited
DK, a Division of Penguin Random House LLC
22 23 24 25 26 10 9 8 7 6 5 4 3 2 1
001–327874–Aug/2022

A catalog record for this book is available from the Library of Congress.
ISBN 978-0-7440-5683-9

DK books are available at special discounts when purchased in bulk for sales
promotions, premiums, fund-raising, or educational use. For details, contact:
DK Publishing Special Markets, 1450 Broadway, Suite 801, New York, NY 10018
SpecialSales@dk.com

Printed and bound in China

For the curious

www.dk.com

This book was made with Forest Stewardship Council ™ certified paper –
one small step in DK's commitment to a sustainable future.
For more information go to **www.dk.com/our-green-pledge**

Contents

Middle Eastern

Middle Eastern and North African cooking is a real-food approach that embraces variety, flavor, and spice drawn from a vast region on the eastern and southern shores of the Mediterranean and beyond. Each country has its own traditions and specialties, with historical influences that can be traced back centuries.

A way of life

As with other parts of the Mediterranean, the food of the Middle East and North Africa is about far more than simple sustenance. It's an integral part of the lifestyle. Preparing and enjoying food is an extension of people's lives, of their families, of their cultures, and of their heritage. And it is reflected in the way they live. It is generous, sociable, and always to be enjoyed surrounded by those you love.

Middle Eastern cooking centers on minimally processed foods such as legumes and whole grains, and plenty of fruit and vegetables, as well as meat, seafood and fish, yogurt, nuts, and seeds. The flavor of food is heightened using warming spices and the addition of a variety of fresh herbs. Also featured are favorites such as extra virgin olive oil, bread, and an assortment of pickled vegetables and condiments such as pomegranate molasses, muhammara, and zhug. These extras always enhance a meal and link all the dishes laid out on the table. In fact, it is rare to see a single dish in isolation—there is always bread, yogurt, or herbs to add depth to a meal.

There are also many health benefits linked with the foods prepared and eaten in the Middle East.

Plant-based sources of protein such as pulses, nuts, and seeds are common throughout the Middle East, while seafood and fish feature in coastal regions. The recipes in this book use oily fish such as sardines and trout; these are good sources of heart-healthy omega-3, which can help to boost brain function, including memory, concentration, and mood.

The Middle Eastern pantry also includes plenty of unrefined whole grains and other fiber-rich foods such as vegetables and fruit. This plant-based focus is a great way to ensure lots of fiber in your diet, fueling your body with naturally slow-burning energy sources. A diet high in fiber is linked to better digestion, as well as more stable moods. Choose whole grains such as quinoa, freekeh, and barley over more refined options. Adding legumes or pulses to your diet will up your fiber intake, too, and help you to stay fuller and more nourished for longer.

Food for the body, food for the soul

Many of the dishes in this book are naturally bright and colorful, thanks to the importance placed on fresh, seasonal produce, as well as the use of fresh herbs, nuts, and seeds. Fresh fruit and vegetables contain plenty of antioxidants and polyphenols, which can help to slow the signs of aging and reduce the risk of inflammatory disease. Filling up on 5–10 servings of vegetables a day is an excellent way to get more antioxidants, polyphenols, vitamins, minerals, and fiber into your diet.

It's not just the type of foods consumed in the Middle East that makes this cooking so good for you. It is the way in which the food is prepared and eaten, with importance placed on mealtimes and sharing.

Meals prepared in these countries are a ritual. Often different elements of a single recipe or entire meal are prepared by multiple members of a family or community who come together to help one another. Most Middle Eastern dishes are designed to be enjoyed with family and friends. This family-style approach to eating food around the table helps to develop a sense of community and connection that is essential to wellbeing and happiness. Sharing foods around the table also helps to foster a healthy relationship with food, where the focus is on enjoyment and satiation, rather than restriction or control. From the kitchen to the table, Middle Eastern food is prepared and eaten thoughtfully and with positive intention.

Traditionally, a large lunch and a lighter dinner are the cornerstones of mealtimes; however, with modern urban life, dinner is often the bigger meal of the day. Eating at the table (and in company) is a simple practice that we can adopt from Middle

Eastern culture, and can promote more mindfulness toward what, when, and how we are eating. Another benefit of eating family-style shared plates is that it encourages a diet of variety. And variety is at the core of Middle Eastern cooking. Mezze, the custom of eating an assortment of small dishes, is a distinct example of this. Eating this way provides a diet that includes a wide range of ingredients, in an array of colors, making it a simple way to help your body get a healthy mix of essential vitamins and minerals.

Transforming everyday eating

There are two principal methods of cooking used: wet and dry. Soups and stews rich with spices are meals in themselves—perfect for breads—while the fierce heat of the grill is used for kefta, skewers, and quick-cooking meat. Larger cuts are cooked slowly in the oven and lend themselves to being partnered with a vegetable or salad dish, or even both.

The Middle Eastern sweet tooth is legendary, with spices, nuts, and the distinctive floral flavors of rosewater and orange blossom imbued into syrups and laced through cakes and pastries.

The Middle Eastern style of eating can help you to live a happier life filled with variety, vitality, and connection through the shared experiences of eating together. The simple approach to cooking, the use of fresh seasonal produce, and the deeply embedded culinary traditions of these cultures make food from the Middle East much loved around the world.

MEZZE

Draw from the complement of vibrant dishes
found here to create inviting morsels ideal
for sharing, from a simple mezze platter
to more elaborate arrays of appetizers.

Persian flatbread with za'atar and roasted grapes

VEGETARIAN | PREP + COOK TIME **1 HOUR + STANDING** | MAKES **3**

A wonderfully versatile Middle Eastern spice mixture, za'atar usually contains sesame seeds, dried wild oregano (also called za'atar) and/or dried thyme, sumac, and salt. It is especially popular as a condiment in Levantine cuisine. Here, we have replaced dried herbs with fresh.

1½ packets (3 tsp) (10g) active dried yeast

1 tsp sugar

⅓ cup (80ml) extra virgin olive oil, divided

3½ cups (450g) bread flour

3 tsp salt flakes

1 lb (450g) red or black seedless grapes

1½ cups (420g) labneh

fresh za'atar

¼ cup (7g) chopped oregano leaves

¼ cup (6g) thyme leaves

2 tbsp white sesame seeds, toasted

2 tbsp black sesame seeds

¼ cup (40g) ground sumac

1 tbsp sea salt flakes

freshly ground black pepper

TIPS

- Store any leftover za'atar in the fridge for up to 3 weeks. Sprinkle on meat, fish, and vegetables before and after grilling or roasting.
- Put each dough portion on a lightly floured sheet of parchment paper when stretching and forming them in step 5. Slide them, still on the parchment, onto the sheets, to make them easier to manage.
- Use a razor blade or very sharp knife to make the incisions in the bread, to avoid dragging the dough and to ensure you cut all the way through.

1 Combine the yeast, 1½ cups (375ml) lukewarm water, and sugar in a small bowl. Allow to stand in a warm place for 10 minutes or until the mixture is frothy. Add 1 tablespoon of the extra virgin olive oil.

2 Put the flour and salt flakes in a large bowl of an electric mixer fitted with a dough hook. Add the yeast mixture. Mix on low speed until just combined. Increase the speed to medium; mix for 10 minutes until the dough is smooth and elastic. Transfer to a large oiled bowl. Loosely cover. Allow to stand in a warm place for 1 hour or until tripled in size.

3 Meanwhile, to make the fresh za'atar, combine the ingredients in a small bowl. Season with pepper to taste.

4 Preheat the oven to 425°F.

5 Tip the dough onto a lightly floured surface without knocking out all of the air. Cut into 3 equal portions. Gently stretch and pat 1 portion into an 4in x 12in oval. Make 2 lengthwise incisions 2in from each end; widen slightly so they don't join together during baking. Repeat with remaining portions. Slide each one onto a baking rack or large sheet to rise. Loosely cover. Stand in a warm place for 40 minutes until puffed and risen.

6 Meanwhile, put the grapes on a baking sheet. Drizzle with 1 tablespoon of the remaining olive oil. Sprinkle with 2 tablespoons of the za'atar. Bake for 15 minutes or until blistered and starting to collapse. Set aside.

7 Increase the oven temperature to 475°F. Place another large baking sheet in the oven to preheat. Working quickly and with 1 portion at a time, brush the dough with some of the remaining olive oil. Slide the dough onto the hot sheet. Sprinkle with 1 tablespoon water. Bake for 5 minutes. Without removing from the oven, sprinkle with 2 teaspoons of the za'atar. Bake for a further 5 minutes. Slide onto a wire rack to cool.

8 Combine the labneh and salt to taste in a small bowl. Top with the grapes and any juices. Serve with the flatbread and a little more of the za'atar.

Crispy za'atar spiced squid

PESCATARIAN | PREP + COOK TIME **40 MINUTES** | SERVES **4**

The lemonlike flavor of za'atar pairs very well with seafood. It adds a delicious zest and brightness to any fish or shellfish. Squid is at its best after brief cooking over high heat, so make this dish just before serving, to keep the squid tender and the coating crisp.

1½ lbs (700g) cleaned squid, hoods only

2 tsp ground white pepper

1 tbsp za'atar

²/₃ cup (100g) brown rice flour

1 cup (70g) fresh whole wheat bread crumbs (use day-old bread to make the crumbs)

¹/₃ cup (15g) finely chopped flat-leaf parsley

4 eggs

¹/₃ cup (80ml) extra virgin olive oil

salt to taste

lemon wedges, to serve

1 Cut the squid in half lengthwise. Score the insides in a crisscross pattern, then cut the squid into 2-in pieces.

2 Combine the white pepper, za'atar, rice flour, bread crumbs, and parsley in a medium bowl. Lightly whisk the eggs in a separate medium bowl. Dip the squid first in the egg, then coat in the bread crumb mixture, shaking off any excess.

3 Heat the olive oil in a large frying pan over medium-high heat. Cook the squid, in batches, for 2 minutes or until golden and just cooked through. Drain on paper towels. Season with sea salt to taste. Serve the squid immediately, with lemon wedges for squeezing over.

Turkish zucchini fritters

VEGETARIAN | PREP + COOK TIME **30 MINUTES** | SERVES **6**

Zucchini fritters, known as mücver, or mücverler, are hugely popular in Turkey both with home cooks and as restaurant fare. The key to getting the exterior of these fritters extra crispy is to ensure that all the excess moisture is removed from the zucchini and carrots.

2 cups (360g) coarsely grated zucchini (about 2 large zucchinis)

2 carrots (240g), coarsely grated

3 greens onions, thinly sliced

2 tbsp coarsely chopped dill, plus extra sprigs, to serve

2 tbsp coarsely chopped flat-leaf parsley

8oz (225g) feta cheese, crumbled

1 tsp sweet paprika

1 1/2 tsp ground cumin

3/4 cup (110g) whole-wheat flour

3 eggs, lightly beaten

sunflower or vegetable oil for frying

salt and freshly ground black pepper

curly endive, to serve

garlic yogurt sauce

1 cup (280g) Greek yogurt

1 tbsp lemon juice

1 small garlic clove, crushed

1 tbsp coarsely chopped dill

1 To make the garlic yogurt sauce, combine the ingredients in a small bowl. Season with salt and pepper to taste. Set aside.

2 Place the zucchini and carrots in a strainer over a bowl. Squeeze the mixture tightly to release the excess liquid and drain. Discard the liquid. Combine the grated vegetables with the green onions, the 2 tablespoons chopped dill, parsley, feta, paprika, cumin, flour, and eggs in a large bowl. Season with salt and pepper to taste. Shape 1/4-cup (60ml) portions of the zucchini mixture into flat rounds to make 12 fritters in total.

3 Heat about 1in of oil in a large skillet over medium heat. Fry the fritters, in batches, for 3 minutes on each side or until lightly browned and cooked through. Drain on paper towels. Serve the fritters with the yogurt sauce, curly endive, and extra dill sprigs. Sprinkle with salt and pepper, if you like.

TIP

These fritters are best made close to serving and served warm.

Eggs with herbs and walnuts

VEGETARIAN | PREP + COOK TIME **40 MINUTES PLUS COOLING** | SERVES **6**

Similar to an Italian frittata, this baked omelet is called "kuku sabzi" in the Middle East, especially in Iran. Full of flavor, it is packed with fresh herbs. For a traditional experience, wrap pieces in a Middle Eastern–style flatbread before dipping in the sauce and eating.

1/4 cup (40g) dried currants

2 tbsp red wine vinegar

1/3 cup (80ml) extra virgin olive oil

1 cup onion (300g), finely chopped

4 garlic cloves, crushed

8 eggs, lightly beaten

1 tsp ground turmeric

1/2 cup (60g) finely chopped walnuts, toasted, plus extra, to serve

3/4 cup (35g) finely chopped flat-leaf parsley, plus extra leaves, to serve

3/4 cup (45g) finely chopped cilantro, plus extra leaves, to serve

3/4 cup (45g) finely chopped dill, plus extra sprigs, to serve

1/4 cup (10g) finely chopped fresh oregano, plus extra sprigs, to serve

salt and freshly ground black pepper

pomegranate seeds, to serve

hummus-yogurt sauce

1/3 cup (90g) hummus

1/3 cup (95g) Greek yogurt

1/2 tsp ground cumin

1 tbsp lemon juice

1 Preheat the oven to 350°F.

2 Combine the currants and vinegar in a small saucepan over medium heat. Bring to a boil; remove from the heat. Set aside to cool.

3 Heat half of the olive oil in a medium skillet over medium-low heat. Cook the onion, stirring, for 5 minutes or until softened. Add the garlic; cook for a further 1 minute or until very soft. Transfer to a bowl to cool. Season well with salt and pepper.

4 Whisk together the eggs, turmeric, cooled currants, walnuts, and herbs in a medium bowl until combined. Season well with salt and pepper.

5 Heat the remaining oil in a large, deep 12in (top measurement) nonstick ovenproof skillet over medium heat. Add the egg mixture; cook over medium-low heat until the edges are starting to set.

6 Transfer the pan to the oven. Bake for 10 minutes or until just set.

7 Meanwhile, to make the hummus-yogurt sauce, combine the ingredients in a small bowl with 1 tablespoon warm water. Season with salt and pepper to taste.

8 Serve the frittata topped with the extra combined herbs, walnuts, and pomegranate seeds. Drizzle with the hummus-yogurt sauce.

TIP

The omelet can be made a day ahead and refrigerated until needed. Allow to come to room temperature before serving.

Mixed mezze

VEGETARIAN | PREP + COOK TIME **35 MINUTES** | SERVES **4–6**

Simple but tempting, this selection of two vegetable dips and accompanying marinated olives is more than the sum of its parts. An ideal mezze platter for informal entertaining or sharing at the end of a long day, it also works well as part of a larger banquet-style meal.

1½ tbsp cumin seeds, toasted

4 garlic cloves, divided, crushed

2 carrots (240g), coarsely grated

⅓ cup (80ml) extra virgin olive oil, divided, plus extra, to serve

¾ cup (175g) coarsely grated raw beets

2 tsp lemon juice, divided

¼ cup (15g) finely chopped mint leaves, plus extra, to serve

⅓ cup (10g) dill, finely chopped, plus extra, to serve

1¼ cups (350g) Greek yogurt, divided

salt and freshly ground black pepper

warmed or chargrilled flatbread, to serve

warm marinated olives

1 garlic clove, crushed

6 strips of lemon zest

2 tsp fennel seeds

½ tsp dried chili pepper flakes

2 tbsp chopped rosemary leaves

⅓ cup (80ml) extra virgin olive oil

2 fresh bay leaves

3 cups (280g) drained mixed black and green olives such as kalamata, Spanish green, and Sicilian

1 To make the vegetable dips, toast half of the cumin seeds in a dry skillet over medium-low heat for 1 minute or until fragrant. Add 4 tablespoons of the olive oil, 2 cloves of garlic, and the carrot. Cook, stirring, for 10 minutes or until the carrot is tender. Season with salt and pepper to taste. Transfer to a medium bowl to cool. Wipe the pan clean. Repeat with the remaining cumin, olive oil, garlic, and the beets.

2 In the bowl of a food processor, combine ¾ cup of the yogurt, 1 teaspoon lemon juice, 2 tablespoons mint leaves, 3 tablespoons dill, and the carrot mixture. Pulse until smooth. Set aside. Repeat with the remaining yogurt, lemon juice, herbs, and the beet mixture. Chill until ready to serve. (The vegetable dips can be made a day ahead, if needed.)

3 To make the warm marinated olives, combine all the ingredients in a small saucepan. Stir over medium-low heat for 3 minutes or until heated through.

4 Serve the carrot and beet dips sprinkled with the extra herbs, accompanied by warmed flatbreads and the warm marinated olives.

TIP

The marinated olives can be stored for 2 weeks in an airtight container in the fridge. The oil will solidify when chilled; to serve, return to a small saucepan and gently warm over a low heat.

Seeded cauliflower keftas with green hummus

VEGETARIAN | PREP + COOK TIME **1 HOUR** | SERVES **6 (MAKES 30 KEFTA)**

While traditional kefta is usually prepared with spiced ground meat such as lamb, beef, or chicken, and often includes other ingredients such as bulgur wheat, this modern version is both vegetarian and vegan-friendly, allowing everyone at the table to enjoy these tasty bites.

½ cup (75g) pumpkin seeds

½ cup (75g) sunflower seeds

¼ cup (40g) sesame seeds

2 tbsp flax seeds

½ cup (12g) firmly packed mint leaves, plus extra, to serve

½ cup (12g) firmly packed flat-leaf parsley leaves, plus extra, to serve

1½ lbs (700g) cauliflower, trimmed, cut into florets

2 garlic cloves, crushed

¼ cup (30g) cumin seeds, toasted, crushed

½ cup (140g) tahini

2 tbsp psyllium husk powder

2 tbsp lemon juice

salt and freshly ground black pepper

peanut oil for deep-frying

green hummus

1 cup (260g) hummus

½ cup (12g) firmly packed mint leaves

½ cup (12g) firmly packed flat-leaf parsley leaves

to serve

lettuce, cherry tomatoes, sliced red onion, cucumber batons, marinated olives (see page 187), feta cheese

1 Preheat the oven to 350°F.

2 To make the green hummus, pulse the hummus, mint, and parsley in a food processor until smooth. Transfer to a bowl and refrigerate until needed.

3 Preheat a medium sauté pan over medium-high heat. Add the pumpkin seeds, sunflower seeds, sesame seeds, and flax seeds. Toast the seeds, stirring, for 2 minutes or until the sesame seeds are golden; be careful not to scorch.

4 Put the toasted seeds, the remaining ingredients (except the peanut oil), and ¼ cup (60ml) water in the bowl of a food processor. Process until the mixture forms a coarse paste. Season well with salt and pepper.

5 Line a baking sheet with parchment paper. Shape heaped tablespoons of the kefta mixture into ovals. Place on the sheet.

6 Fill a medium saucepan two-thirds full with peanut oil. Heat to 325°F (or until the oil sizzles when a small cube of bread is added). Working in batches of 6 at a time, fry the keftas for 5 minutes or until dark golden and cooked through. Remove with a slotted spoon. Drain on paper towels.

7 Serve the keftas with the green hummus, lettuce, tomato, onion, cucumber, olives, and feta cheese.

TIP

The recipe can be prepared a day ahead up to the end of step 6.

Carrot falafel

VEGETARIAN | PREP + COOK TIME **30 MINUTES** | MAKES **28**

Team this delectable version of the almost ubiquitous falafel with chickpea tabbouleh (see page 32), green hummus (page 20), muhammara (page 186), and warm flatbread for a heartier meal, or use as a finger food for a mezze-style selection of appetizers.

1 cup (240g) coarsely grated carrots

1/4 cup (80g) finely chopped red onion

1 x 15oz (425g) can chickpeas, drained, rinsed

1 tsp ground cumin

2 tsp harissa paste (see tips)

1/4 cup (35g) all-purpose flour

1/2 tsp baking powder

1 egg

1 1/2 cups (110g) panko bread crumbs, divided

vegetable oil for frying

salt and freshly ground black pepper

Greek yogurt, to serve

lemon wedges, to serve

1 Process the carrot, onion, chickpeas, cumin, and harissa paste in a food processor until finely chopped. Add the flour, baking powder, and egg, then season with salt and pepper to taste. Process until the mixture just comes together.

2 Transfer the carrot mixture to a large bowl. Stir in $^3/_4$ cup (55g) of the bread crumbs. Roll level tablespoons of the mixture into balls (it should make about 28 falafel). Transfer to a baking sheet. Roll the falafel in the remaining bread crumbs to coat.

3 Fill a large saucepan or wok one-third full of vegetable oil, and heat to 350°F (or until a cube of bread browns in 15 seconds). Fry the falafel, in batches, for 2 minutes or until golden and cooked through. Drain on paper towels.

4 Serve the falafel with yogurt and lemon wedges for squeezing over.

TIPS

- Falafel can be prepared a day ahead. Roll in the remaining bread crumbs just before cooking.
- Harissa paste is a condiment made with red chiles, garlic, oil, and often vinegar or lemon to provide acidity. You can use ready-made harissa paste or make your own using the recipe on page 186.

Tomato, merguez sausage, and pine nut stew

PREP + COOK TIME **35 MINUTES** | SERVES **4**

Fiery, spice-filled merguez sausages provide an extra kick of heat to this hearty tomato-based stew. Merguez is traditionally made with lamb or beef, or a mixture of both. Serve the stew with a variety of mezze dishes and plenty of flatbread to mop up the juices.

1 tbsp extra virgin olive oil

$\frac{1}{2}$ cup (150g) finely chopped onion

1 garlic clove, crushed

1 long red chile, finely chopped

1 x 8oz (225g) jar piquillo peppers, drained, finely chopped

2 x 14.5oz cans (822g) cans diced tomatoes

1 cup (250ml) vegetable stock

2 x 15oz cans (850g) chickpeas, drained, rinsed

2 fresh merguez sausages (160g)

$\frac{1}{4}$ cup (40g) pine nuts, toasted

salt and freshly ground black pepper

1 Heat the oil in a large saucepan over medium-high heat; add the onion, garlic, and chile. Cook, stirring, for 5 minutes or until softened. Add the piquillo peppers. Continue to cook, stirring, for a further 5 minutes.

2 Add canned tomatoes, stock, and chickpeas. Bring to a boil, then reduce the heat. Simmer for 15 minutes or until reduced slightly.

3 Meanwhile, slice the sausages lengthwise. Heat a ridged cast-iron grill pan over medium heat. Cook the sausages, turning once, for 7 minutes or until charred and cooked through. Drain on paper towels.

4 Serve the stew topped with the sausages and toasted pine nuts.

5 Season with salt and pepper to taste.

TIP

Merguez sausages are popular in North Africa, especially in the cuisines of Morocco, Tunisia, and Algeria. Available fresh and sometimes dried, these harissa-spiked sausages are used in grilled and couscous-based dishes, as well as in tagines.

Labneh

Labneh is thick, strained yogurt used as a spread, dip, or accompaniment, often seasoned with salt and lemon juice. Always part of a traditional mezze spread, labneh is eaten for breakfast, lunch, and dinner, and in desserts as a tangy alternative to cream. You can find it in your local grocery store, or you can make your own. Drain the yogurt for even longer to make a fresh cheese that can be formed into balls and flavored in oil with herbs, or rolled in spices.

Basic labneh

VEGETARIAN | PREP TIME **5 MINUTES + 24 HOURS' REFRIGERATION**
MAKES **1 CUP**

Place a strainer over a medium bowl. Line with cheesecloth. Spoon 2 cups (560g) Greek yogurt into the cloth. Gather into a ball; secure with string or a rubber band. Refrigerate for 24 hours or until thickened. Transfer the labneh to a small airtight container. Label and date. Keep refrigerated for up to 2 weeks.
TIP Save the drained liquid (whey) to use in smoothies or add to soups. For vanilla-flavored labneh, stir the scraped seeds from 1 vanilla pod into the labneh at the end.

Labneh cheese balls

VEGETARIAN | PREP TIME **20 MINUTES + 48 HOURS' REFRIGERATION**
MAKES **12 BALLS (250G)**

Place a strainer over a medium bowl. Line with cheesecloth. Stir together 2 cups (560g) Greek yogurt and 1½ teaspoons salt in a small bowl. Spoon into the cloth. Gather into a ball; secure with string or a rubber band. Refrigerate for 48 hours or until very thick. (The longer the yogurt is left to drain, the firmer the resulting labneh will be.) Using oiled hands, roll heaped tablespoonfuls of the labneh into balls. Place in a 3-cup (750ml) jar. Pour over 2 cups (500ml) light olive oil. Label and date. Keep refrigerated for up to 2 months. To eat, remove the labneh from the olive oil, and serve in salads or spread onto bread.

Coated labneh cheese balls

VEGETARIAN | PREP TIME **20 MINUTES (+ PRIOR 48 HOURS' REFRIGERATION)** | MAKES **12 BALLS (250G)**

Remove the labneh cheese balls (see left) from the olive oil and roll in one of the following coatings. Labneh balls are best coated close to using, or keep refrigerated for up to 3 days.

Fresh herbs Combine 2 tablespoons each of finely chopped flat-leaf parsley, cilantro, and dill with 1 teaspoon sumac in a small bowl. Roll the labneh balls in the mixture.

Spicy Combine 2 tablespoons sweet paprika, 1 teaspoon dried chili pepper flakes, and 2 teaspoons finely grated lemon zest in a small bowl. Roll the labneh balls in the mixture.

Traditional Za'atar Roll the labneh balls in 3–4 tablespoons za'atar.

Traditional Dukkah Roll the labneh balls in ½ cup (45g) ready-made dukkah.

Spicy grilled shrimp with freekeh and eggplant

PESCATARIAN | PREP + COOK TIME **1 HOUR** | SERVES **4**

This appealing Middle Eastern–inspired grain bowl can be enjoyed at lunch or dinner. Freekeh adds its singular nutlike flavor, providing a foil for the other layers of flavor. For an equally inviting twist, swap the shrimp for salmon.

4oz (120g) freekeh, rinsed

1¼ lb (600g) eggplant, cut into 2 inch pieces

extra virgin olive oil cooking spray

1 tsp dried chili pepper flakes

1 garlic clove, crushed

1 tsp extra virgin olive oil

1 lb (450g) raw shrimp, deveined, tails intact

1 x 15oz (425g) can chickpeas, drained, rinsed

¼ cup (80g) thinly sliced red onion

½ cup (10g) small basil leaves

freshly ground black pepper

roasted tomato dressing

8oz (225g) cherry vine tomatoes, halved

1 tsp dried chili pepper flakes

2 garlic cloves, sliced

1 tsp extra virgin olive oil

2 tsp white balsamic vinegar

1 tsp finely grated lemon zest

1 tbsp lemon juice

TIPS

• Freekeh, made from green durum wheat, is a long-used staple in the Middle East and North Africa. Its name comes from the threshing process used to prepare it. The wheat is harvested while still soft, then roasted, rubbed, and dried, before being cracked like bulgur wheat.

• The water content in tomatoes can vary, so simply add a little water to the dressing if it's too thick.

1 Preheat the oven to 425°F. Cook the freekeh in a medium saucepan of boiling water for 35 minutes or until tender. Drain well. Transfer to a large bowl; set aside.

2 Meanwhile, line 2 large baking sheets with parchment paper. Arrange the eggplant pieces on one sheet; spray with the cooking spray. Place on the top shelf of the oven. Roast the eggplant, turning occasionally, for 30 minutes or until golden and tender.

3 To make the roasted tomato dressing, put the tomatoes, chili pepper flakes, and sliced garlic on the second lined sheet; drizzle with the olive oil. Season with pepper to taste. Place on the middle shelf of the oven. Roast the tomatoes for 10 minutes or until the garlic is golden. Transfer the garlic to a plate; reserve. Roast the tomatoes for a further 10 minutes or until collapsed.

4 Combine the shrimp, chili, garlic, and olive oil in a medium bowl.

5 To finish the roasted tomato dressing, in a food processor bowl, combine the roasted tomatoes and reserved garlic, white balsamic vinegar, lemon zest, and lemon juice. Process until smooth. Season with pepper to taste. Set aside.

6 Preheat a lightly oiled ridged cast-iron grill pan or outdoor grill to a high heat. Cook the shrimp for 1 minute on each side or until just cooked.

7 Add the chickpeas, onion, roasted eggplant, and basil to the freekeh in the bowl. Toss to combine. Divide the freekeh salad and shrimp among 4 serving plates. Serve drizzled with the roasted tomato dressing.

Lentil and sumac phyllo rolls

VEGETARIAN | PREP + COOK TIME **45 MINUTES** | MAKES **8**

For a toothsome handheld snack to eat on the go, these rolls are the perfect size to pack for your lunch for work or school. It goes without saying, they are also perfect served as an element of a mezze-style meal with accompanying dips and condiments.

2 x 14oz cans (794g) cans brown lentils, drained, rinsed

1/4 cup (80g) finely grated onion

2 garlic cloves, crushed

1/3 cup (45g) chopped roasted pistachios

1 tsp sweet paprika

1 tsp ground cumin

1/4 tsp ground cinnamon

1/4 tsp dried chili pepper flakes

1 egg, lightly beaten

10 phyllo pastry sheets, thawed if frozen

extra virgin olive oil cooking spray

1/4 tsp sumac

salt and freshly ground black pepper

harissa yogurt (see page 42), to serve

spicy marinated olives (see page 187), to serve

1 Preheat the oven to 400°F. Line a large baking sheet with parchment paper.

2 Put the lentils in a large bowl. Mash lightly. Add the onion, garlic, pistachios, spices, and beaten egg. Stir to combine. Season with salt and pepper to taste.

3 Layer 5 sheets of the phyllo dough on a clean, dry surface, spraying each sheet with a little of the olive oil cooking spray. While you work, keep the remaining sheets covered with parchment paper, topped with a clean, damp dish towel to prevent drying out. Place half of the lentil mixture along one long side of the phyllo. Roll to enclose the filling. Cut into 4 even lengths. Place on the prepared sheet. Spray with olive oil. Repeat with the remaining phyllo sheets, olive oil, and lentil mixture to make 8 rolls in total. Sprinkle with the sumac.

4 Bake the phyllo pastry rolls for 30 minutes or until golden. Serve with the harissa yogurt and spicy marinated olives.

Chickpea tabbouleh

VEGETARIAN/VEGAN | PREP + COOK TIME **15 MINUTES** | SERVES **4 AS A SIDE**

Tabbouleh is so easy to make you'll consider never buying it ready-made again. It's great to have on hand, to accompany a multitude of Middle Eastern–inspired meat and vegetable dishes. Chickpeas are added here, but fresh herbs and zingy tomato are still the focus.

1/4 cup (50g) coarse bulgur wheat

3 tomatoes (450g)

1 x 15oz (425g) can chickpeas, drained, rinsed

3 green onions, finely chopped

2 cups (60g) coarsely chopped flat-leaf parsley

1/4 cup (15g) coarsely chopped mint leaves

1/4 cup (60ml) extra virgin olive oil

1/4 cup (60ml) lemon juice

1 Put the bulgur wheat and 1/4 cup (60ml) boiling water in a small heatproof bowl. Cover with plastic wrap. Allow to stand for 10 minutes or until the water is absorbed.

2 Meanwhile, remove the seeds from the tomatoes. Finely chop the flesh. Pulse the chickpeas in a food processor until coarsely chopped.

3 Put the bulgur wheat, chopped tomato, and chickpeas in a large bowl with the green onions, parsley, mint, olive oil, and lemon juice. Toss gently to combine.

TIPS

- You can easily double the quantities in this recipe if you are feeding more people.
- When making ahead, add the oil and lemon juice close to serving.
- If you like, add some finely chopped cucumber and finely chopped red onion to the tabbouleh.

Savory baklava with haloumi and pistachios

VEGETARIAN | PREP + COOK TIME **1 HOUR 30 MINUTES + COOLING** | SERVES **8**

This nutty, cheesy savory version of the traditionally sweet spiced baklava is best served warm. Pistachio nuts still feature in the filling, but the usual cinnamon is paired with cumin and lemon thyme; haloumi and feta cheeses add a salty counterpoint to the honey syrup.

1 cup (140g) shelled pistachios

1 cup (100g) walnuts

1 tsp ground cinnamon

2 tsp ground cumin

2 tbsp extra virgin olive oil

1/2 cup (150g), finely chopped

4 garlic cloves, crushed

8 oz (225g) haloumi cheese, grated

8 oz (225g) feta cheese, crumbled

1 tbsp finely grated lemon zest

1 tbsp chopped lemon thyme leaves, plus extra 2 sprigs for the syrup

1 cup (250g) butter, melted, plus extra for greasing

18 phyllo pastry sheets, thawed if frozen

1/4 cup (90g) honey

2 tbsp lemon juice

salt and freshly ground black pepper

1 Preheat the oven to 350°F. Spray a 9in x 9in baking dish with cooking spray. Line with parchment paper, extending the paper above the sides.

2 On a large baking sheet, combine the pistachios and walnuts. Toss them in the cinnamon and cumin. Bake for 10 minutes or until the nuts are golden. Let cool. Finely chop the nuts. Set aside.

3 Heat the olive oil in a medium sauté pan over medium-low heat. Add the onion and garlic. Cook, stirring, for 8 minutes or until softened. Set aside to cool.

4 In a large bowl, combine the haloumi and feta cheeses, lemon zest, chopped lemon thyme, and nut and onion mixtures in a large bowl. Season with salt and pepper to taste.

5 Reserve 1/4 cup (50g) of the melted butter. In the baking dish, layer 3 pastry sheets, evenly brushing each with a little of the remaining melted butter. Fold in half crosswise. (Keep the remaining phyllo covered with parchment paper and topped with a damp paper towel to prevent drying out.) Brush with butter; tuck in the edges. Evenly sprinkle with a loosely packed cup of haloumi cheese mixture.

6 Layer 2 more folded pastry sheets, brushing each with butter. Place over the mixture in the pan, tucking in the edges. Sprinkle with 1 cup of the haloumi cheese mixture. Repeat 5 more times. Finish with 3 layers of phyllo, folded in half crosswise. Brush well with butter.

7 Using a sharp knife, cut the baklava into 1–1 1/2in diamonds. Bake for 45 minutes or until the pastry is golden and crisp.

8 Meanwhile, to make the syrup, heat the reserved butter in a small pan over high heat. Cook, swirling the pan occasionally, until well browned. Add the honey, lemon juice, and thyme sprigs. Reduce the heat to low. Cook, stirring, for 2 minutes until melted and combined; discard thyme.

9 Brush the baklava with some of the syrup. Drizzle with the rest to serve.

Spiced lamb and stuffed grape leaves

PREP + COOK TIME **1 HOUR 25 MINUTES + COOLING** | MAKES **22**

Many versions of stuffed grape vine leaves are found across the Middle East and Mediterranean. Instead of an herbed rice mixture, we've prepared a lamb and barley version with the dried figs and ras el hanout, a North African spice blend used in Moroccan, Tunisian, and Algerian cuisine. Look for it in the spice aisle or specialty section.

¹⁄₄ cup (60ml) extra virgin olive oil, divided

¹⁄₄ cup (80g) finely chopped onion

4 garlic cloves, crushed

¹⁄₂ lb (250g) ground lamb

1¹⁄₂ tbsp ras el hanout

1¹⁄₂ tbsp pine nuts, toasted

2 tbsp lemon juice

3oz (75g) soft dried figs, stems removed, finely chopped

¹⁄₃ cup (65g) pearl barley

1 cup (25g) firmly packed flat-leaf parsley leaves, finely chopped

33 large preserved grape leaves (165g)

1 small lemon (65g), thinly sliced

olive oil cooking spray

salt and freshly ground black pepper

hummus and Greek yogurt, to serve

1 Heat 2 tablespoons of the olive oil in a medium skillet over medium heat. Cook the onion and garlic, stirring, for 5 minutes or until soft. Season well with salt and pepper. Add the lamb and ras el hanout; cook, stirring to break up any lumps, for 5 minutes or until cooked. Stir in the pine nuts, lemon juice, dried figs, pearl barley, and parsley. Allow to cool slightly.

2 Rinse the grape leaves. Scald in a large saucepan of boiling water, in batches, for 1 minute. Transfer the leaves to a colander. Rinse under cold running water, then drain well. Place a grape leaf, smooth-side down, on a clean work surface; trim the large stem. Place 1 tablespoon of the lamb mixture in the center. Fold the stem end and sides of the grape leaf over the filling; roll up firmly. Repeat with more leaves and the remaining lamb mixture to make 22 rolls in total.

3 Spray a 9in round heavy-based sauté pan with olive oil cooking spray; line with the remaining grape leaves. Position the rolls in the pan, seam-side down, in a single layer, packing in closely. Top with the lemon slices. Pour 1¹⁄₄ cups (310ml) water and the remaining olive oil over the rolls. Place an inverted 6in plate on top of the rolls to secure. Cover the pan with a lid. Simmer, covered, over a low heat for 1 hour or until the leaves and pearl barley are tender. Remove from the heat; take the lid off the pan. Allow to cool for 30 minutes.

4 Serve the stuffed grape leaves accompanied by hummus and yogurt.

Middle Eastern deviled eggs with crispy pita bread and pickled peppers

VEGETARIAN | PREP + COOK TIME **35 MINUTES + STANDING** | SERVES **4**

We've put a Middle Eastern–flavored spin on everyone's favorite deviled egg. Flavored with cumin, peppers, smoky eggplant, and sumac, these delicious treats make it hard to stop at one! Serve these as a snack or appetizer.

You will need to start this recipe at least 6 hours ahead

6 eggs, at room temperature

2 large pita breads (160g), split

1/4 cup (60ml) extra virgin olive oil

1 garlic clove, halved

1 tbsp cumin seeds, roughly crushed

2 tbsp sesame seeds, toasted

1/2 cup (240g) ready-made baba ghanoush

1/4 tsp chili pepper flakes

1 tsp ground sumac

2 tbsp cilantro leaves

salt and freshly ground black pepper

pink pickled turnips (see page 187), to serve

pickled chillies

10 chile peppers, halved lengthwise

2/3 cup (160ml) apple cider vinegar

1 tbsp cumin seeds, toasted

1 tbsp sea salt flakes

TIPS

- Instead of using a food processor in step 6, you can mix the ingredients with a fork.
- Pickled peppers can be made 2 weeks ahead. Refrigerate until needed.
- Crispy pita bread can be made 2 days ahead.

1. To make the pickled peppers, combine the ingredients in a bowl, making sure the peppers are covered with liquid. Allow to stand at room temperature for 6 hours or overnight. (For longer periods, store, covered, in the fridge.) Before serving, remove the peppers from the pickling liquid.

2. Preheat the oven to 350°F.

3. Cook the eggs in a medium saucepan of boiling water for 9 minutes for hard-boiled. Drain. Allow to cool in cold water, then peel the eggs, slice in half, and scoop out the cooked yolks. Set the eggs and yolks aside separately.

4. Meanwhile, brush the insides of the pockets inside the pita bread with the olive oil and rub with a cut side of the garlic. Sprinkle with the cumin. Place on 2 large baking sheets. Bake for 8 minutes, rotating the sheets if needed, or until browned and crisp. When cool, break into shards. Set aside.

5. Put the sesame seeds in a small bowl. Cut the eggs in half lengthwise. Using a small spoon, scoop the egg yolks into a medium bowl. Dip the cut surface of the whites onto the sesame seeds to cover. Place on a sheet.

6. In a food processor, add the egg yolks, baba ghanoush, and chili pepper flakes and process until smooth. Season with salt and pepper to taste. Spoon the mixture into a piping bag fitted with a 2in plain nozzle. Pipe the filling into the egg halves. Sprinkle with the sumac.

7. Serve the deviled eggs with the cilantro, pickled peppers, crispy pita bread, and pickled turnips.

Goat cheese and za'atar stuffed baby sweet peppers

VEGETARIAN | PREP + COOK TIME **30 MINUTES** | SERVES **6**

Small in size but big on flavor, these sweet pepper bites can be served as a small plate as part of a mezze-style meal or as part of a grazing board. The earthy flavor of the za'atar, with its citrus undertones, complements the creamy-textured cheese and roasted peppers.

8oz (225g) goat cheese, softened

2 tbsp za'atar, lightly toasted, plus extra, to serve (optional)

1 tbsp honey

2 tsp finely grated lemon zest

3/4 lb (350g) baby sweet peppers, halved lengthwise

1/4 cup (60ml) extra virgin olive oil, divided

1 tbsp lemon juice

1/2 cup (20g) small cilantro leaves

1/2 cup (12g) small mint leaves

2 tbsp flaked almonds, toasted

salt and freshly ground black pepper

1 Preheat the oven to 400°F. Line a large baking sheet with parchment paper.

2 Combine the goat cheese, za'atar, honey, and lemon zest in a small bowl until smooth. Spoon the mixture into a piping bag fitted with a 2in plain nozzle. Set aside.

3 Using a small spoon, remove the seeds and membranes from the pepper halves; discard. Place the peppers on the prepared sheet, drizzle with 1 tablespoon of the olive oil. Season with salt and pepper to taste. Bake for 15 minutes or until caramelized at the edges and tender.

4 Meanwhile, combine the remaining oil and the lemon juice in a small bowl. Season with salt and pepper to taste. Add the cilantro and mint. Toss gently to combine.

5 Arrange the peppers on a serving platter. Pipe even amounts of the cheese mixture into each half. Top with the almonds. Serve with the herb salad, sprinkled with extra toasted za'atar, if you like.

Zucchini keftas with harissa yogurt

PREP + COOK TIME **45 MINUTES** | SERVES **4**

These croquette-style keftas, with their soft, velvety interior and crispy golden coating, are enlivened with chile pepper and lemon zest. Of course, the accompanying harissa yogurt for dipping enlivens them even further!

$^1/_2$ lb (250g) russet potatoes, scrubbed, peeled, halved

3 cups (500g) coarsely grated zucchini (about 3 large zucchini)

1 long green chile, finely chopped

2 tsp finely grated lemon zest

4 green onions, finely chopped

$^1/_2$ cup (80g) rice flour

sunflower or other vegetable oil for frying

salt and freshly ground black pepper

lemon wedges, to serve

harissa yogurt

2 tsp harissa paste, or to taste

1 tsp smoked paprika

1 garlic clove, crushed

$^1/_2$ cup (140g) Greek yogurt

1 Put the potatoes in a small saucepan with enough cold water to cover. Bring to a boil. Cook for 25 minutes or until tender. Drain. Return to the pan. Coarsely mash with a fork.

2 Meanwhile, to make the harissa yogurt, combine the ingredients in a small bowl. Season with salt and pepper to taste.

3 In a strainer over a bowl, squeeze the zucchini tightly to eliminate excess moisture. Discard the liquid. Combine the zucchini, chile pepper, lemon zest, green onions, mashed potatoes, and rice flour in a large bowl. Season with salt and pepper to taste. Shape $^1/_4$-cup measures of the zucchini mixture into ovals to make 12 keftas in total.

4 Heat enough sunflower oil to come to a depth of 1in in a large frying pan over high heat. Fry the kefta, in batches, for 3 minutes on each side or until golden and crisp. Remove with a slotted spoon. Drain on paper towels.

5 Serve the keftas with the harissa yogurt and lemon wedges for squeezing over. Sprinkle with salt, if you like.

TIPS

- The harissa yogurt can be made 2 days ahead; store, covered, in the fridge until ready to serve.
- Serve the keftas and harissa yogurt in wraps with salad leaves for a more substantial meal.

Beef, haloumi cheese, and spinach borek

PREP + COOK TIME **1 HOUR 20 MINUTES + COOLING** | SERVES **4**

Borek is a filled pastry found across parts of the Middle East, Europe, and into the Caucasus, a legacy with roots in its popularity during the time of the Ottoman Empire. Traditionally made with thin, flaky pastry, it features a variety of fillings such as meat, egg, vegetable, or cheese.

$^1/_3$ cup (80ml) extra virgin olive oil, divided

$^1/_2$ cup (150g) finely chopped onion

2 garlic cloves, crushed

$^3/_4$ lb (300g) ground beef

1 x 14.5oz (411g) can diced tomatoes

2 tbsp tomato paste

1 tbsp Worcestershire sauce

$^1/_2$ cup (125ml) beef stock

2 tbsp chopped thyme leaves, plus extra sprigs, to serve

6 phyllo pastry sheets, thawed if frozen

8oz (225g) haloumi cheese, coarsely grated

$^1/_2$ cup (25g) firmly packed baby spinach leaves

salt and freshly ground black pepper

baby kale leaves and lemon wedges, to serve

1 Heat 1 tablespoon of the olive oil in a large, deep frying pan over medium heat. Cook the onion, stirring, for 5 minutes or until soft. Add the garlic and beef. Cook, stirring to break up any lumps, for 5 minutes or until the beef is browned. Stir in the diced tomatoes, tomato paste, Worcestershire sauce, beef stock, and the 2 tablespoons chopped thyme. Bring to a boil. Reduce the heat to low. Simmer, partially covered, for 45 minutes or until thickened. Season with salt and pepper to taste. Allow to cool.

2 Preheat the oven to 400°F. On a large piece of parchment paper, layer the phyllo sheets on top of each other, brushing with some of the remaining oil between each layer. Spread the beef filling over one half of the pastry, leaving a 1in border. Evenly top with the haloumi cheese and spinach. Fold the pastry over the filling, then fold over the edges to secure. Slide the pastry on the parchment paper onto a large baking sheet. Brush the pastry with a little more oil, then sprinkle with the extra thyme sprigs and cracked black pepper to taste.

3 Bake for 25 minutes or until golden and crisp. Cut into pieces, and serve with the baby kale and lemon wedges for squeezing over.

TIPS

- Borek is best baked just before serving.
- The beef filling can be made up to 2 days ahead. Store, covered, in the fridge until needed.

Mezze menu

Mezze is a quintessential part of Middle Eastern cuisine. The practice is found in varied forms across the Middle East and North Africa, but invariably at its heart is an inclusive attitude toward food and eating. Comprising of a selection of small dishes such as dips, pickles, meat, vegetables, and pastries, the custom invites many to gather around the table to share and enjoy a meal.

MEZZE RECIPES

VEGETABLES AND SALADS

Fresh, seasonal vegetables star here. With dishes ranging from classic shakshuka to zesty salads brimful of appeal, you will be spoiled for choice at any time of the year.

Shakshuka with Brussels sprouts, olives, and labneh

VEGETARIAN | PREP + COOK TIME **30 MINUTES + STANDING** | SERVES **4**

A classic dish from the Maghreb region of North Africa, shakshuka has spread to become a brunch-time meal the world over. The eggs are traditionally cooked in a spiced-tomato-and-pepper-based sauce, but this modern twist uses Brussels sprouts, kale, and green olives.

$1/3$ cup (80ml) extra virgin olive oil, divided

10oz (300g) small Brussels sprouts, halved

1 cup (300g) thinly sliced leeks (about 3 leeks)

2 garlic cloves, crushed

1 bunch (150g) kale, coarsely chopped

$1/2$ cup (125ml) vegetable stock

8 eggs

$1/4$ cup (60g) pitted green olives, chopped

$1/4$ cup (7g) chopped flat-leaf parsley

2 tsp finely grated lemon zest

$1/2$ cup (125g) labneh (see page 26)

salt and freshly ground black pepper

1 Heat 5 tablespoons of the olive oil in a large heavy-based ovenproof frying pan over medium heat. Cook the Brussels sprouts, stirring, until browned and almost tender. Add the leek, garlic, and kale; cook, stirring occasionally, for 5 minutes or until the vegetables soften. Stir in the vegetable stock. Bring to a simmer.

2 Using the back of a spoon, make 8 shallow indentations in the mixture. Break 1 egg into each hollow. Place the pan under the broiler for 6–8 minutes until the egg whites are set and the yolks remain runny, or until cooked to your liking.

3 Meanwhile, combine the olives, parsley, lemon zest, and remaining olive oil in a small bowl. Season with salt and pepper to taste.

4 Top the shakshuka with the labneh and the olive mixture. Season with salt and pepper to taste. Serve immediately.

TIPS

- You can use Swiss chard or extra spinach instead of the kale, if you like.
- This recipe is best made just before serving.

Farro, haloumi cheese, and chickpea salad

VEGETARIAN | PREP + COOK TIME **1 HOUR 5 MINUTES** | SERVES **4**

A nutty whole grain, farro is the term used collectively for three ancient and long-used types of wheat and is often added to soups or salads. Here, you can swap the haloumi cheese for another protein such as chicken, lamb, or fish, or even soft-boiled eggs.

1 cup (195g) roasted farro

8oz (225g) haloumi cheese

1 tbsp extra virgin olive oil

6 soft fresh dates such as medjool (120g), pitted, torn

2 cucumbers (260g), thinly sliced lengthwise

1/4 cup (80g) thinly sliced red onion

2 cups (50g) firmly packed flat-leaf parsley leaves

1 x 15oz (425g) can chickpeas, drained, rinsed

1/3 cup (70g) pomegranate seeds

1/4 cup (40g) pine nuts, toasted

salt and freshly ground black pepper

lemon-oregano dressing

1 tbsp lemon juice

1/4 cup (60ml) white wine vinegar

1 garlic clove, crushed

1 tsp dried oregano

1/2 cup (125ml) extra virgin olive oil

1 Put the farro and 6 cups (1.5 liters) water in a large saucepan. Bring to a boil. Reduce the heat to low. Cook, covered, for 45 minutes or until tender. Drain. Rinse under cold running water. Drain well.

2 Meanwhile, to make the lemon-oregano dressing, blend or process the lemon juice, vinegar, garlic, and oregano until well combined. With the motor operating, gradually add the olive oil until the dressing is creamy and combined. Season with salt and pepper to taste. Set aside.

3 Cut the haloumi cheese horizontally into slices 2in thick. Cut each slice into 2 triangles. Heat the olive oil in a large frying pan over high heat. Cook the haloumi cheese for 1 minute on each side or until golden.

4 Combine the farro, dates, cucumbers, onion, parsley, chickpeas, and lemon-oregano dressing in a large serving bowl. Season with salt and pepper to taste. Top with the haloumi cheese triangles. Sprinkle with the pomegranate seeds and pine nuts, and serve.

TIPS

- If the dressing separates on standing, blend again briefly to bring it together.
- You can use crumbled feta cheese instead of haloumi cheese.
- The farro can be cooked and the dressing made a day ahead. The salad itself is best assembled just before serving.
- Haloumi cheese is always best eaten warm, as it can be rubbery when cold.

SERVING SUGGESTION Serve with Chargrilled Chicken with Fig and Olive Sauce (see page 99).

Carrot, Brussels sprouts, and cumin phyllo pie with tahini cream

VEGETARIAN/VEGAN | PREP + COOK TIME **1 HOUR + COOLING** | SERVES **6**

Rolling and coiling the pastry for this pie is not as difficult as it seems. We recommend you use fresh phyllo pastry sheets from the refrigerated section of the supermarket, as these tend to be less brittle than frozen phyllo and are therefore easier to work with.

$^1/_2$ cup (125ml) extra virgin olive oil, divided

$1^1/_2$ cups (450g) thinly sliced leek, white part only

3 garlic cloves, crushed

2 tsp cumin seeds

$1^1/_4$ cup (380g) coarsely grated carrots

$^3/_4$ lb (375g) Brussels sprouts, trimmed, shredded

$^1/_3$ cup (55g) dried currants

$^1/_3$ cup (16g) finely chopped mint

14 phyllo pastry sheets, thawed if frozen

ground sumac, to sprinkle

crunchy seed topping

$^1/_4$ cup (50g) pumpkin seeds

$^1/_4$ cup (35g) slivered almonds

$^1/_4$ cup (25g) coarsely chopped walnuts

1 tbsp poppy seeds

1 tbsp sesame seeds

tahini cream

$^1/_4$ cup (60g) tahini

2 tbsp lemon juice

$^1/_4$ cup (60ml) cold tap water

salt and freshly ground black pepper

1 Heat $^1/_3$ cup (80ml) of the olive oil in a large frying pan over medium heat; cook the leek, garlic, and cumin seeds for 5 minutes. Add the carrot; cook for 3 minutes. Add the Brussels sprouts; cook for a further 5 minutes or until the vegetables are soft. Stir in the currants and mint. Set aside to cool.

2 Meanwhile, to make the crunchy seed topping, combine the ingredients in a small bowl. Set aside.

3 Preheat the oven to 350°F.

4 Divide the filling into 7 portions. Brush 1 sheet of the phyllo pastry with a little of the remaining olive oil; top with a second sheet. Keep the remaining sheets covered with parchment paper topped with a damp paper towel to prevent them from drying out. Place 1 portion of the filling lengthwise, in a thin line, along the pastry edge; roll the pastry over the filling. Starting at the center of a 9in springform pan, carefully form the pastry roll, seam-side down, into a coil. Repeat with the remaining pastry sheets, olive oil, and filling, joining each roll to the end of the last one and coiling it around until the bottom of the pan is covered. Brush the top with a little more of the olive oil.

5 Bake the phyllo pie for 20 minutes. Cover the pie evenly with the crunchy seed topping; bake for a further 10 minutes or until golden.

6 Meanwhile, make the tahini cream. Combine the tahini and lemon juice in a small bowl; whisk in the cold water until smooth. Season with salt and pepper to taste.

7 Serve the phyllo pie with the tahini cream, topped with a little sumac.

Tomato tagine with nutty couscous

VEGETARIAN/VEGAN | PREP + COOK TIME **45 MINUTES** | SERVES **4**

This wonderful recipe combines to form a mouthwatering melange of tastes, aromas, and cooking methods of the Middle East and North Africa. Indeed, couscous is such a part of the fabric of daily life in North Africa that it is considered part of its cultural heritage.

1³/₄ lb (800g) tomatoes

4 garlic cloves, unpeeled

1 cup (300g) thin wedges of red onion

¹/₃ cup (80ml) extra virgin olive oil

2 tsp ground cumin

2 tsp ground coriander

1 tsp ground ginger

2 tsp sweet paprika

1 tsp sea salt flakes

¹/₄ cup (7g) coarsely chopped flat-leaf parsley

nutty couscous

¹/₂ cup (45g) sliced almonds

4 tbsp (50g) butter, diced

1¹/₂ cups (300g) wholegrain couscous

1¹/₂ cups (375ml) vegetable stock

1 Preheat the oven to 350°F. Line a large baking sheet with parchment paper.

2 Cut any small tomatoes in half. Cut the larger tomatoes into quarters or wedges. Remove the seeds. Smash the garlic cloves with the flat side of a knife, leaving the skins on. Put the tomatoes on the baking sheet, followed by the garlic and red onion.

3 Combine the olive oil, all of the spices, and salt in a small bowl. Pour over the tomatoes. Roast for 25 minutes or until the tomatoes are soft, but still retain their shape.

4 Meanwhile, make the nutty couscous. Put the almonds and butter in a medium saucepan over medium heat. Cook, stirring occasionally, for 2 minutes or until the nuts are golden. Add the couscous. Stir for 1 minute or until the couscous is heated through. Transfer to a large heatproof bowl. In the same pan, bring the vegetable stock to a boil. Pour the stock over the couscous. Cover with plastic wrap. Let stand for 10 minutes, then fluff the grains of couscous with a fork.

5 Stir half of the parsley through the tomato mixture. Spoon the couscous into a large serving bowl; top with the tomato tagine. Serve sprinkled with the remaining parsley.

TIP

This recipe can be made a day ahead. Store the tomato tagine and couscous in separate airtight containers in the fridge.

Baked feta with herbed orange and endive salad

VEGETARIAN | PREP + COOK TIME **35 MINUTES** | SERVES **4**

While feta cheese doesn't melt when heated (as the acid content is too high), roasting this cheese makes for a wonderfully soft, tender texture that is a delicious contrast to the crunchy, slightly bitter endive leaves used here.

2 x 8oz (550g) blocks of feta cheese

2 tbsp honey, divided

1/2 cup (125ml) extra virgin olive oil, divided

1/4 cup (60ml) apple cider vinegar

1 tbsp coriander seeds, toasted, lightly crushed

1/4 tsp chili pepper flakes

3 white endive heads (375g), leaves separated

3 large navel oranges (900g), peeled, thinly sliced

1 1/2 cups (400g), thinly sliced celery, sliced on the diagonal, young leaves reserved

1/2 cup (50g) walnuts, roasted, coarsely chopped

salt and freshly ground black pepper

1 Preheat the oven to 400°F. Line a baking sheet with parchment paper.

2 Pat the feta cheese dry with paper towels. Place on the lined baking sheet. Combine 1 tablespoon of the honey and 1 tablespoon of the olive oil in a small bowl. Spread evenly over the feta cheese; season with pepper to taste. Bake for 20 minutes or until the feta cheese is soft and golden.

3 Meanwhile, whisk together the remaining 1 tablespoon honey, remaining olive oil, vinegar, coriander seeds, and chili pepper flakes in a medium bowl until well combined. Season with salt and pepper to taste.

4 Halve the larger leaves of the endive lengthwise. Arrange the endive leaves, orange slices, celery slices, and reserved celery leaves on a large platter, then drizzle with half of the dressing. Toss gently to combine.

5 To serve, top the salad with the walnuts and roughly broken pieces of the warm baked feta cheese. Drizzle with the remaining dressing.

TIPS

- Radicchio, or curly endive, would also work well in this recipe.
- Add some finely chopped cilantro and dill to the dressing in step 3, if you like.

Kabocha squash fatteh with almond tarator sauce

VEGETARIAN/VEGAN | PREP + COOK TIME **45 MINUTES** | SERVES **4**

Popular in many cuisines, fatteh is fresh or toasted flatbread covered with other ingredients, in this case squash. The tarator sauce is a twist on Turkish tarator using almonds instead of walnuts (or tahini found in other regions).

2 lbs (800g) kabocha squash (Japanese pumpkin) unpeeled, cut into thick wedges

1/4 cup (60ml) extra virgin olive oil, divided

1 1/2 tbsp za'atar

1 lb (450g) red peppers, thickly sliced

1 red onion (170g), thickly sliced

1 large whole wheat pita bread split into two rounds

1 x 15 oz can (425g) can chickpeas, drained, rinsed

2 tbsp pine nuts, toasted

1/3 cup (7g) flat-leaf parsley leaves

1/3 cup (7g) mint leaves

salt and freshly ground black pepper

lemon wedges, to serve

almond tarator

1 cup (160g) blanched almonds, roasted

2 garlic cloves, crushed

1 cup (70g) coarsely chopped day-old bread

2 tbsp white wine vinegar

1/3 cup (80ml) extra virgin olive oil

1 Preheat the oven to 425°F. Line 2 large baking sheets with parchment paper.

2 Arrange the pumpkin wedges on one of the lined sheets. Drizzle with 1 tablespoon of the olive oil, then sprinkle with 1 tablespoon of the za'atar. Season with salt and pepper to taste. Roast for 30 minutes or until just tender. At the same time, arrange the peppers and onion on the second lined sheet. Drizzle with another tablespoon of the extra virgin olive oil, then season with salt and pepper to taste. Roast for 20 minutes or until tender.

3 Place the bread on a third, unlined baking sheet, lightly brush with the remaining olive oil. Season with salt and pepper to taste. Toast the bread in the oven for 3 minutes or until crisp. Allow to cool, then tear into pieces. Set aside.

4 In the bowl of a food processor, add the almonds, garlic, bread, and vinegar until wet bread crumbs form. With the motor running, gradually add the olive oil in a thin, steady stream until combined. Add 1/2 cup (125ml) water; process until the mixture is smooth. Season with salt and pepper to taste.

5 Arrange the roasted vegetables on a platter with the chickpeas, pine nuts, parsley, and mint. Top with the remaining 1/2 tablespoon za'atar. Serve with the toasted bread, accompanied by the tarator and lemon wedges for squeezing over.

TIPS

• For an extra nutty salad, swap the chickpeas for roasted pistachios and almonds, if you like.

• You can assemble the salad ahead of time, without the bread. When ready, scatter the bread over the salad or simply serve it on the side.

Smoky eggplant with sumac onions

VEGETARIAN | PREP + COOK TIME **45 MINUTES PLUS COOLING** | SERVES **4**

This recipe is a modern interpretation of the classic Middle Eastern dip baba ghanoush, which combines charred eggplant, tahini, and garlic. The Lebanese-style tarator here is a more traditional one, with yogurt instead of water to thin the sauce. Serve as a small shared plate.

1/3 cup (100g) thinly sliced red onion

1 tbsp lemon juice

1 tsp sumac, divided

1¼ lb (600g) eggplant

2 tbsp extra virgin olive oil

salt and freshly ground black pepper

toasted bread slices, to serve

tarator sauce

1 tbsp tahini

1 garlic clove, crushed

1 tbsp lemon juice

2/3 cup (190g) Greek yogurt

1 Preheat a ridged cast-iron grill pan or grill to high heat. Combine the onion, lemon juice, and 1/2 teaspoon of the sumac in a small bowl. Set aside.

2 Prick the eggplants all over with a fork; leave the stems intact. Cook on the barbecue, turning occasionally, for 30 minutes or until the skin is charred and the flesh is very tender. Place the eggplants in a large strainer over a large bowl to drain. Allow to cool.

3 Meanwhile, to make the sauce, combine the tahini, garlic, lemon juice, and yogurt in a small bowl. Season with salt and pepper to taste.

4 Remove and discard the skin from the eggplants, keeping the tops still intact. Halve the flesh and arrange on a serving plate. Season well with salt and pepper. Drizzle the eggplant with the olive oil. Spoon the yogurt sauce over the eggplants; top with the onion mixture and the remaining 1/2 teaspoon sumac. Serve with toasted bread.

TIPS

▪ The onion mixture, grilled eggplant, and tahini mixture can all be made a day ahead. Refrigerate in separate containers. Bring to room temperature before combining and serving.

▪ Eggplant is one of those rare vegetables that can't be eaten raw, as it is just not palatable unless cooked. Make sure you cook it until it is very tender and season it well.

Sumac root vegetables with lentils, pickled red onion, and mint

VEGETARIAN/VEGAN | PREP + COOK TIME **1 HOUR 10 MINUTES** | SERVES **4**

This dish is a lovely accompaniment to roast or grilled chicken or lamb, but its complexity of flavors also makes it a dish that stands on its own. Roasting the root vegetables brings out their natural sugars, while the sumac imparts its characteristic tang and lemony acidity.

1³/₄ lb (800g) celery root, peeled, cut into 2 in pieces

1 lb (450g) small parsnips, peeled, halved lengthwise

2 lbs (1kg) rutabagas, peeled, cut into ¹/₂ in rounds

¹/₄ cup (60ml) extra virgin olive oil

1 tbsp ground sumac

1 cup (200g) Puy or other green lentils, uncooked, rinsed

¹/₂ cup (125ml) white wine vinegar

1 tbsp sugar

1¹/₂ tsp salt

2 cups (600g) thinly sliced red onions

¹/₃ cup (45g) pistachios, roasted

¹/₄ cup (40g) almonds, roasted, coarsely chopped

¹/₂ cup (75g) pomegranate seeds

salt and freshly ground black pepper

mint dressing

2 tbsp white wine vinegar

¹/₂ cup (125ml) extra virgin olive oil

¹/₄ cup (60ml) lemon juice

1 cup (50g) shredded mint leaves

1 Preheat the oven to 400°F. Line two large baking sheets with parchment paper.

2 Arrange the vegetables on the baking sheets in a single layer. Combine the olive oil and sumac in a small bowl. Season with salt and pepper to taste. Brush the oil mixture over the vegetables. Roast for 45 minutes or until golden and tender.

3 Meanwhile, cook the lentils in a medium saucepan of boiling water for 25 minutes or until just tender; drain. Rinse under cold running water, draining well.

4 Put the white wine vinegar, sugar, and 1¹/₂ teaspoons salt in a medium bowl. Stir until the sugar dissolves. Add the red onions. Stir to combine. Set aside, stirring occasionally, to lightly pickle. Drain just before serving.

5 To make the mint dressing, put the ingredients in a screw-top jar with a tight-fitting lid. Shake well. Season with salt and pepper to taste.

6 Place the lentils on a large platter. Top with the roasted vegetables, pickled onion, pistachios, almonds, and pomegranate seeds. Drizzle with the mint dressing, then season with salt and pepper to taste. Toss gently to combine.

Pickled fennel and fig salad with cinnamon dressing

VEGETARIAN/VEGAN | PREP + COOK TIME **25 MINUTES** | SERVES **6 AS A SIDE**

Cinnamon adds a wonderful warmth and fragrant perfume to any dish in which it is used, whether sweet or savory. Here, it is blended into the simple citrussy dressing, completely transforming the flavor of this humble salad.

$\frac{1}{2}$ cup (125ml) apple cider vinegar

$\frac{1}{4}$ cup (55g) sugar

1 tsp salt

1$\frac{1}{4}$ cups (390g) shaved fennel, fronds reserved

1 lb (450g) small radishes, trimmed, quartered

1$\frac{1}{2}$ tbsp extra virgin olive oil

1 x 14oz (397g) can brown lentils, drained, rinsed, patted dry

6 small purple figs (250g), halved or quartered

$\frac{1}{2}$ cup (10g) flat-leaf parsley leaves

$\frac{1}{2}$ cup (10g) mint leaves

salt and freshly ground black pepper

cinnamon dressing

1 tsp ground cinnamon

2 tsp cumin seeds, toasted

$\frac{1}{4}$ cup (60ml) extra virgin olive oil

1$\frac{1}{2}$ tbsp lemon juice

1 Put the vinegar, sugar, and the 1 teaspoon salt in a medium bowl. Season well with pepper. Stir until the sugar has dissolved. Add the fennel and radishes. Stir to combine. Allow to stand for 15 minutes to lightly pickle. Drain, reserving the pickling liquid.

2 Meanwhile, heat the oil in a medium frying pan over medium-high heat. Add the lentils. Cook, covered, shaking the pan occasionally, for 7 minutes or until crisp. Drain on paper towels. Season with salt and pepper to taste.

3 To make the cinnamon dressing, whisk together the ingredients in a medium jug with 1$\frac{1}{2}$ tablespoons of the reserved pickling liquid to combine. Season with salt and pepper to taste.

4 Arrange the pickled fennel and radishes, crispy lentils, figs, parsley, mint, and reserved fennel fronds on a large platter. Drizzle with the cinnamon dressing. Toss gently to combine.

Roasted colorful beet and labneh salad

VEGETARIAN | PREP + COOK TIME **1 HOUR 15 MINUTES** | SERVES **4**

This simple root vegetable is elevated into a sophisticated salad by using a variety of beets to create an assortment of colors and textures. Serve the salad with slices of toasted Turkish pide bread or pita bread, if you like, to mop up any juices.

2 lbs (1kg) large red beets, trimmed, peeled, cut into wedges

2 tsp fennel seeds

^{1}/$_4$ cup (60ml) extra virgin olive oil, divided

1 lb (450g) baby red beets, trimmed and scrubbed

1^1/$_4$ lb (600g) golden beets, trimmed, scrubbed

2 tbsp pistachios, finely chopped

2 tsp finely grated lemon zest

1 tbsp lemon juice, divided

1 lb (450g) small Chioggia beets, trimmed, scrubbed, thinly sliced

1^1/$_2$ cups (420g) labneh (see tips)

salt and freshly ground black pepper

pita or flatbread slices, toasted, to serve (optional)

1   Preheat the oven to 400°F. Line two large baking sheets with parchment paper.

2   Place the large beet wedges on one of the baking sheets. Sprinkle with half of the fennel seeds. Drizzle with 1 tablespoon of the olive oil. Season with salt and pepper to taste. Place the smaller red and golden beets on the second lined sheet. Sprinkle with the remaining fennel seeds and another 1 tablespoon of the olive oil. Season with salt and pepper to taste. Put both trays in the oven. Bake the smaller beets for 45 minutes or until tender. Bake the larger beet wedges for a further 15 minutes or until tender. When cool enough to handle, cut the smaller whole beets into quarters.

3   Meanwhile, in a food processor, chop the pistachios until very finely ground. Set aside.

4   Whisk together the remaining olive oil, 1 teaspoon of the lemon zest, and the lemon juice in a small bowl. Season with salt and pepper to taste.

5   Arrange the roasted beets, Chioggia slices, and spoonfuls of labneh on a large platter, with the toasted bread on the side, if using. Drizzle over the dressing, and sprinkle with the ground pistachios and remaining 1 teaspoon lemon zest.

TIPS

▪ Use a mandoline or V-slicer to slice the Chioggia beets very thinly. Chioggia beets, also known as candy-stripe or bull's-eye beets, are an Italian heirloom variety that has characteristic rings when cut horizontally.

▪ If making your own labneh, you will need to prepare it at least a day ahead of serving the salad, Follow the basic labneh recipe on page 26, using 3 cups (840g) Greek yogurt to yield the 1^1/$_2$ cups (420g) labneh that is needed here.

Spiced eggplant and giant couscous salad

VEGETARIAN | PREP + COOK TIME **1 HOUR 5 MINUTES** | SERVES **4**

Despite the name, Israeli giant (or pearl) couscous—known as *ptitim* in Israel—is not actually a type of couscous, but rather a tiny pasta ball made of toasted semolina. Developed in the mid 20th century as an alternative to rice, it has become a much-loved staple.

2 tbsp cumin seeds

1 tbsp fennel seeds

1 tsp chili pepper flakes

1¼ lb (600g) eggplant, halved lengthwise

⅓ cup (80ml) extra virgin olive oil, divided

1 cup (170g) Israeli couscous or pearl couscous (moghrabieh) (see tips)

1 x 15oz (425g) can chickpeas, drained, rinsed

½ cup (75g) pomegranate seeds

1 cup (30g) chopped flat-leaf parsley leaves

2 tbsp lemon juice, divided

¾ cup (200g) Greek yogurt

1 tbsp tahini

1 tbsp pomegranate molasses

salt and freshly ground black pepper

1 Preheat the oven to 400°F. Line a large baking sheet with parchment paper.

2 Toast the cumin seeds, fennel seeds, and chili pepper flakes in a small skillet over medium heat for 1 minute or until fragrant. Transfer to a spice grinder, or use a mortar and pestle. Blend or crush until finely ground.

3 Using a sharp knife, score the flesh of the eggplants ½in deep to form a diamond pattern. Arrange the eggplants, cut-side up, on the lined baking sheet. Brush with ¼ cup (60ml) of the olive oil, then sprinkle with 2 tablespoons of the spice mix. Season with salt and pepper to taste. Bake for 45 minutes or until tender and golden.

4 Cook the pearl couscous in a large saucepan of boiling water for 6 minutes or until just tender. Drain. Rinse under cold running water, drain well. Transfer to a medium bowl. Add the chickpeas, pomegranate seeds, parsley, 1 tablespoon of the lemon juice, and the remaining olive oil. Season with salt and pepper to taste. Toss gently to combine.

5 Combine the yogurt, tahini, and remaining 1 tablespoon lemon juice in a small bowl. Season with salt and pepper to taste.

6 Serve the spiced eggplant topped with the couscous salad and yogurt mixture, and drizzled with the pomegranate molasses.

TIPS

▪ The toasted spice mix makes about ¼ cup (30g). You can sprinkle the salad with some of the remaining spice mix, or store it for up to 2 weeks in an airtight container. Sprinkle on flatbreads, dips, or grilled or roasted meat and fish.

▪ Popular as an ingredient and as a dish of the same name in Lebanon, Jordan, and Syria, moghrabieh is very similar to Israeli couscous. Slightly larger in size, it has a longer history in Levantine cuisine.

Spiced carrot salad

VEGETARIAN | PREP + COOK TIME **30 MINUTES** | SERVES **4**

The humble carrot is transformed in this salad reminiscent of the classic Moroccan dish, and enriched by the addition of fragrant spices including cumin, coriander, and cardamom. The toasted spices are used to make a citrus-based dressing that draws all the flavors together.

1/4 cup (40g) dried currants

1/4 cup (60ml) red wine vinegar

1 tsp brown mustard seeds

1 tsp cumin seeds

1 tsp coriander seeds

1/2 tsp cardamom seeds (use the seeds of 10 green cardamom pods)

4 tbsp (60g) butter

1 1/2 cups (480g) grated carrots

3 tsp finely chopped fresh root ginger

1/2 lb (250g) baby rainbow carrots, cut into ribbons

1/3 cup (40g) flaked almonds, toasted

1 cup (30g) cilantro leaves

1/4 cup (60ml) olive oil

2 tbsp orange juice

2 tsp honey

salt and freshly ground black pepper

slices of warmed flatbread such as pita pocket bread, to serve (optional)

1 Combine the currants and vinegar in a small microwave-safe bowl. Microwave on medium (80%) for 1 minute or until hot. Set aside to cool.

2 Meanwhile, toast the seeds in a small skillet over medium heat for 1 minute or until fragrant. Transfer to a spice grinder, or use a mortar and pestle. Blend or crush until finely ground. Set aside.

3 Melt the butter in a small saucepan over high heat. Add the grated carrot and ginger. Cook, stirring, for 2 minutes until light golden. Reduce the heat to low. Cook, covered, for a further 5 minutes or until softened. Transfer to a food processor. Pulse until smooth. Season with salt and pepper to taste. Set aside.

4 Drain the currants (reserve the liquid). Combine the drained currants, carrot ribbons, toasted almonds, and cilantro in a medium bowl. Whisk together the reserved currant liquid with the olive oil, orange juice, honey, and finely ground spices in a small bowl until combined. Pour the dressing over the carrot salad. Season with salt and pepper to taste. Toss to combine.

5 Spread the carrot purée on a serving platter. Top with the carrot salad. Serve with the warmed flatbread, if you like.

TIP

Use a vegetable peeler, mandoline, or V-slicer to cut the baby carrots into ribbons.

Chargrilled mushroom, broccolini, and freekeh salad

VEGETARIAN | PREP + COOK TIME **30 MINUTES** | SERVES **4**

Similar in texture to bulgur wheat, freekeh is made from young, green wheat grains. These are roasted or smoked, then polished to remove the tough outer bran, before being cracked to use as a side dish like rice or added to anything from soups to salads. Preserved lemons are a North African specialty and add a wonderful citrus perfume to any dish.

1 cup (200g) freekeh, rinsed

1 lb (450g) portobello mushrooms

5oz (150g) oyster mushrooms, large ones halved

6oz (175g) broccolini

$\frac{1}{2}$ cup (125ml) extra virgin olive oil, divided

3 garlic cloves, crushed

1 tsp ground sumac

1 tsp finely grated lemon zest

2 tbsp lemon juice

3 cups (120g) arugula

5oz feta cheese, drained

2 wedges of preserved lemon (80g), pulp removed and discarded, rind thinly sliced (see tip)

$\frac{1}{4}$ cup (40g) pine nuts, toasted

salt and freshly ground black pepper

1. Cook the freekeh in a large saucepan of boiling water for 10 minutes or until just tender. Drain well. Let cool.

2. Meanwhile, preheat a ridged grill-pan or grill to high heat. Put the mushrooms, broccolini, $\frac{1}{3}$ cup (80ml) of the olive oil, 2 of the crushed garlic cloves, and the sumac in a large bowl. Season with salt and pepper to taste. Toss to coat.

3. Cook the flat mushrooms for 2 minutes on each side or until charred and tender. Remove from the pan and set aside. Cook the oyster mushrooms for 30 seconds on each side or until charred and tender. Remove from the pan and set aside. Cook the broccolini for 1 minute on each side or until charred and tender.

4. To make the dressing, combine the grated lemon zest, lemon juice, remaining crushed garlic, and remaining olive oil in a small bowl.

5. Put the freekeh, mushrooms, and broccolini in a large bowl with the arugula, crumbled feta cheese, preserved lemon zest, pine nuts, and dressing. Season with salt and pepper to taste. Toss gently to combine.

TIPS

- Preserved lemons are available in jars from quality supermarkets and specialty stores. If you want to make your own, use the recipe on page 187.
- Usually, only the rind of preserved lemon is used in cooking, as in the recipe here. To prepare, remove and discard the pulp from the lemon wedges. Squeeze out any juice in the rind, then rinse well to reduce saltiness. Thinly slice or cut as directed in the recipe.

Shirazi cucumber salad with yogurt dressing and crisp fava beans

VEGETARIAN | PREP + COOK TIME **40 MINUTES** | SERVES **6 AS PART OF A BANQUET**

This simple salad with Persian roots will create more liquid as it stands. This can be seen only as a bonus because it creates delicious juices that can be mopped up with warmed pita bread, making for a very satisfying meal.

1 x 15oz (426g) fava beans, drained, patted dry

1 tsp salt

1 tsp ground cumin

$^1/_4$ cup (60ml) extra virgin olive oil, divided

1 large lemon (200g)

$^3/_4$ cup (200g) Greek yogurt

2 garlic cloves, crushed

3 lbs (1.2kg) English or European cucumbers

1 cup (300g) thinly sliced celery

2 red chile peppers, seeded, finely chopped

$^1/_2$ cup (25g) finely chopped mint leaves, plus extra small leaves, to serve

2 tsp ground sumac

salt and freshly ground black pepper

1 Preheat the oven to 400°F. Line a large baking sheet with parchment paper.

2 Combine the fava beans, salt, cumin, and 1 tablespoon of the olive oil in a bowl. Spread out over the lined sheet. Roast in the oven, stirring halfway through the cooking time, for 30 minutes or until crisp and golden. Allow to cool.

3 Meanwhile, finely grate the zest from the lemon (see tips), then squeeze out the juice.

4 In a small bowl, combine the yogurt, garlic, and 2$^1/_2$ tablespoons of the lemon juice (reserve the rest of the juice for the salad). Season with salt and pepper to taste. Set aside.

5 Chop the cucumbers into random chunks and slices. Put in a large bowl with the celery, chiles, lemon zest, chopped mint, remaining olive oil, and reserved lemon juice. Season lightly with salt and pepper to taste. Toss gently to combine.

6 Arrange the cucumber salad on a serving platter. Top with the roasted fava beans and yogurt dressing. Sprinkle with the sumac, then top with extra mint leaves.

TIPS

- Canned fava beans are available at most large supermarkets and Middle Eastern grocers.
- If you have one, use a zester to remove the lemon zest in thin strips.

Turkish braised fava beans and shallots

VEGETARIAN | PREP + COOK TIME **1 HOUR** | SERVES **6**

Saffron, the much-prized spice derived from the *Crocus sativus* flower, is revered not only for the vivid yellow color it adds to food, but also most notably for its unrivaled floral perfume. Follow the Turkish tradition and use fresh fava beans when they are in season.

1 tsp saffron threads

1/2 cup (125ml) extra virgin olive oil, divided

8 large shallots (480g), peeled, whole

1 medium garlic bulb, cloves separated, peeled

1/2 lb (225g) vine-ripened tomatoes, seeds removed, coarsely chopped

2 lbs (1kg) fava beans, fresh or frozen, thawed, skins removed from half (see tip)

4 cups (1 liter) vegetable stock

8oz (225g) pita pocket bread

1 tbsp dukkah (see tip)

1/4 cup (7g) fresh dill, chopped, plus extra sprigs, to serve

2 tsp finely grated lemon zest

1/4 cup (60ml) lemon juice

1/2 cup (55g) coarsely chopped roasted walnuts

salt and freshly ground black pepper

Greek yogurt, to serve

1 Preheat the oven to 400°F. Line a baking sheet with parchment paper.

2 Combine the saffron and 1 tablespoon of boiling water in a small cup. Let stand for 10 minutes.

3 Heat 1/4 cup (60ml) of the olive oil in a large deep ovenproof skillet over medium heat. Cook the shallots and garlic, stirring occasionally, for 4 minutes or until starting to caramelize. Add the tomatoes.

4 Cook, stirring, for 1 minute or until fragrant. Add the unpeeled fava beans, vegetable stock, and saffron mixture to the pan. Bring to a boil. Transfer to the oven. Bake for 45 minutes or until the shallots are very soft and the sauce is slightly reduced.

5 Meanwhile, drizzle the cut sides of the bread with the remaining oil. Sprinkle with the dukkah, then season with salt and pepper to taste. Place on the lined baking sheet. Toast in the oven for the last 15 minutes of the bean mixture's cooking time or until golden and crisp.

6 Place the baked bean mixture in a large serving dish with the peeled fava beans, chopped dill, lemon zest, and lemon juice. Stir to combine. Season with salt and pepper to taste. Top with the walnuts and extra dill sprigs.

7 Serve with the toasted bread and yogurt.

TIP

Fava beans are available both fresh and frozen. To use fresh fava beans, remove them from the pod, then remove the outer long green pod (shell). Then blanch the beans to easily peel away the beige-green skin. Frozen fava beans have already had their pods removed, but still retain the beige skin. Fava beans can be eaten with the skin still on or peeled off.

Crispy seed-and-spice Middle Eastern potatoes

VEGETARIAN/VEGAN | PREP + COOK TIME **55 MINUTES** | SERVES **4**

These Lebanese-style potatoes known as *batata harra*, with their dukkahlike coating, are twice-cooked to achieve a perfect texture. First boiled until tender, then deep-fried until crispy, they have a crunchy outside and fluffy inside—and a taste that is hard to resist.

3¹/₂ lbs (1.6 kg) russet potatoes, scrubbed, unpeeled, cut into 2 in chunks

1 garlic bulb, cloves separated, unpeeled

1 tbsp coriander seeds

1 tbsp cumin seeds

2 tsp white sesame seeds

2 tsp black sesame seeds

3 tsp salt

1 tsp smoked paprika

¹/₂ tsp chili pepper flakes

6 cups (1.5 liters) vegetable oil for deep-frying

¹/₂ cup (20g) finely chopped flat-leaf parsley

1 tbsp finely grated lemon zest

1 Put the potatoes and garlic in a large saucepan with enough cold salted water to cover. Bring to a boil, covered, over high heat. Reduce the heat. Simmer, uncovered, for 15 minutes or until tender and the potato skins are just starting to loosen. Drain in a colander. Remove the garlic. Peel away the skin from the cloves and set aside. Allow the potatoes to stand for 5 minutes to steam dry. Toss the potatoes in the colander a few times to roughen the edges slightly.

2 Meanwhile, toast the seeds in a medium frying pan over medium heat, stirring often, for 6 minutes or until fragrant. Transfer to a mortar; allow to cool for 5 minutes. Using a pestle, pound the seeds until coarsely ground. Stir in the sea salt, paprika, and chili pepper flakes. Set aside.

3 Heat the oil in a deep heavy-based saucepan over medium heat until it reaches 350°F (or until a cube of bread dropped into the oil turns brown in 30 seconds). Cook the potatoes and garlic, in batches and turning halfway through the cooking time, for 10 minutes; remove the garlic after 3 minutes or when very golden and crisp.

4 Using a slotted spoon, transfer the garlic and potatoes to a large bowl. Add the seed mixture, parsley, and lemon zest. Toss gently to combine.

TIP

Try chunks of sweet potato for something different. Adjust the cooking time accordingly.

Grilled cauliflower with hazelnut sauce

VEGETARIAN/VEGAN | PREP + COOK TIME **55 MINUTES** | SERVES **6**

Roasting the cauliflower at a very high temperature creates a heavenly caramelized crust around the edges, contrasting beautifully with the tender flesh inside. The lightly pickled grapes add a nice pop of sweetness and acidity to the dish.

1 x 3 lb (1.5kg) head of cauliflower

¼ cup (60ml) extra virgin olive oil, plus extra 2 tsp

2 garlic cloves, crushed

2 tsp smoked paprika

1 tsp ground cumin

2 shallots (50g), thinly sliced

½ lb (225g) seedless red grapes, halved

2 tsp sherry vinegar

⅓ cup (50g) skinless toasted hazelnuts, coarsely chopped

¼ cup (7g) fresh oregano leaves

salt and freshly ground black pepper

hazelnut sauce

1 cup (50g) chopped sourdough bread, crusts removed

1¼ cups (170g) skinless toasted hazelnuts

¼ cup (60ml) extra virgin olive oil

1 small garlic clove, crushed

2 tbsp sherry vinegar

1 To make the hazelnut sauce, put the bread and 1 cup (250ml) water in a medium bowl. Allow to stand for 5 minutes. Squeeze out any excess water from the bread; transfer to a blender with the hazelnuts, olive oil, and garlic. With the motor running, slowly stream in up to 1 cup (250ml) extra water, blending until a very smooth sauce forms. Stir in the sherry vinegar. Season with salt and pepper to taste. Refrigerate until ready to serve.

2 Preheat the oven to 475°F. Line a large baking sheet with parchment paper.

3 Break the cauliflower into large florets. Put the cauliflower on the lined baking sheet.

4 Combine the ¼ cup (60ml) olive oil, garlic, paprika, and cumin in a small bowl. Pour the mixture over the cauliflower; toss to coat. Arrange the cauliflower in a single layer on the baking sheet. Set aside for 15 minutes to allow the flavors to infuse.

5 Season the cauliflower with salt and pepper to taste. Roast in the oven for 25 minutes or until golden and tender.

6 Meanwhile, combine the shallots, grapes, the extra 2 teaspoons olive oil, and vinegar in a medium bowl. Season with salt and pepper to taste. Set aside for 10 minutes to allow to pickle slightly.

7 Divide the hazelnut sauce among 6 serving plates. Top with the cauliflower, and sprinkle with the hazelnuts and oregano. Serve with the grape salad alongside.

TIP

The hazelnut sauce can be made up to a day ahead, while the cauliflower can be marinated a day ahead. The flavor will intensify with time. Store in separate containers in the fridge until needed.

Herbed freekeh salad with salmon and labneh

PESCATARIAN | PREP + COOK TIME **1 HOUR + OVERNIGHT REFRIGERATION** | SERVES **4**

Making your own labneh is not difficult—just remember to allow enough time for overnight straining. Using hot-smoked salmon creates a speedy and easy meal to put together on the day. You can swap hot-smoked salmon for pan-fried fresh salmon or any other fish, if you like.

You will need to start this recipe a day ahead

16oz (550g) Greek yogurt

1 cup (200g) freekeh, rinsed

1/4 cup (80g) thinly sliced red onion

1 cup (300g) thinly sliced red bell pepper

1 cup (20g) mint leaves, large leaves sliced

1 cup (30g) small basil leaves

1 cup (20g) flat-leaf parsley leaves

2 tbsp pitted kalamata olives, finely chopped

2/3 cup (100g) pomegranate seeds (see tips)

1 1/2 tbsp extra virgin olive oil

2 tbsp lemon juice

5oz (150g) hot-smoked salmon

1 Line a strainer with 2 layers of cheesecloth. Place the strainer over a deep bowl. Spoon the yogurt into the strainer, gather the cloth, and tie into a ball with kitchen string or a rubber band. Refrigerate for 24 hours or until thick.

2 Meanwhile, cook the freekeh according to the package instructions. Drain well. Allow to cool. Combine the freekeh, onion, red pepper, herbs, and olives. Reserve half of the pomegranate seeds; crush the remaining seeds to release their juice. Put 1 tablespoon of the pomegranate juice with the olive oil and lemon juice in a screw-top jar with a tight-fitting lid. Shake well. Pour the dressing over the salad, and toss well.

3 Remove the skin from the salmon and flake into rough chunks. Top the freekeh salad with the salmon, small spoonfuls of the labneh, and the reserved pomegranate seeds.

TIPS

- You will need about 1 large pomegranate for this recipe.
- The drained liquid (whey) from the labneh can be used in smoothies and soups. It will keep for about 3 days in the fridge. You can also use ready-made labneh, if you like.

Banquet menu

In the Middle East, sharing food around the table is about more than the simple act of eating. It is about communion, the bringing together of family and friends in acknowledgment of the emotional and social bonds that interweave our daily lives. This simple banquet-style meal with its accompanying condiments and bread encourages this, built as it is with dishes made for sharing and savoring.

BANQUET RECIPES

ROASTS
AND GRILLS

Indoor eating, outdoor eating, family nights in, weekend entertaining—choose from these succulent roasts and smoky, flavor-packed grills for the ideal dish for any occasion.

Roasted Middle Eastern mixed seafood

PESCATARIAN | PREP + COOK TIME **45 MINUTES** | SERVES **4**

Ras el hanout is a popular spice mix used in Morocco, Tunisia, and Algeria. Its translation from Arabic means "head of the shop," referencing the best spices the merchant has to offer. Exact blends can vary from merchant to merchant, and even from family to family.

2 tbsp ras el hanout

2 garlic cloves, crushed

¹⁄₃ cup (80ml) extra virgin olive oil

3 x 8oz (225g) sea bream fillets, skin on, pin-boned, halved

1 lb (500g) fresh mussels, scrubbed, beards removed

1 lb (450g) large tiger shrimp, peeled and deveined

¹⁄₂ lb (225g) cherry tomatoes, cut into clusters

¹⁄₃ cup (10g) cilantro

salt and freshly ground black pepper

warmed flatbread, to serve (optional)

cucumber yogurt

1 cup (250g) Greek yogurt

¹⁄₂ cup (150g) finely chopped cucumber

1 Preheat the oven to 425°F. Line two large baking sheets with parchment paper.

2 Combine the ras el hanout, garlic, and ¹⁄₄ cup (60ml) of the olive oil in a large bowl. Season with salt and black pepper to taste. Add the seafood. Toss well to coat. Divide the seafood evenly between the prepared baking sheets. Top with the tomatoes, and drizzle with the remaining olive oil.

3 Roast the seafood mixture in the oven for 20 minutes or until the fish and shrimp are just cooked through, the mussels open, and the tomato skins are just starting to split.

4 Meanwhile, to make the cucumber yogurt, combine the yogurt and half of the cucumber in a small bowl. Top with the remaining cucumber. Season with salt and pepper to taste.

5 Top the seafood mixture with the cilantro. Serve with the cucumber yogurt and warmed flatbread, if you like.

TIPS

- Check the seafood after 3 minutes of roasting and remove any mussels that have already opened. Some mussels might not open after cooking—these may not have cooked as quickly as the others—and some will not open even after excessive cooking.
- You can use another firm white fish instead of the sea bream, such as sea bass or snapper, and use clams or cockles instead of the mussels, if you like.

Baked sardines with fig and pine nut stuffing

PESCATARIAN | PREP + COOK TIME **1 HOUR** | SERVES **6**

This recipe uses fresh sardines, which taste moist, tender, and sweet compared to their common salty canned counterpart. Dried fruits are frequently used in Middle Eastern and North African dishes, and here dried figs add their own sweetness to the stuffing.

²/₃ cup (130g) chopped dried figs

¹/₃ cup (80ml) red wine vinegar

¹/₃ cup (80ml) extra virgin olive oil, divided

1 cup (70g) coarse day-old sourdough bread crumbs

¹/₂ cup (150g) finely chopped onion

2 garlic cloves, crushed

2 tsp finely grated lemon zest

2 tbsp finely chopped rosemary, plus extra 2 tbsp leaves

2 tbsp finely chopped flat-leaf parsley

2 tbsp pine nuts, toasted

1 tbsp lemon juice

1¼ lb (600g) fresh sardines (about 12), cleaned, with head and tails intact (see tips)

1 fennel bulb (300g), trimmed, sliced, fronds reserved

1 radicchio (200g), cut into 12 wedges

2 tbsp vincotto, divided (see tips)

salt and freshly ground black pepper

lemon wedges, to serve

TIPS

- Ask your fishmonger to clean the sardines for you.
- Italian vincotto, literally meaning "cooked wine," is a condiment made from boiling down grape must (skins, seeds, and stems) until thick and syrupy. It is available from selected supermarkets and delis. You can use balsamic glaze instead, if you like.

1 Preheat the oven to 400°F. Oil and line a roasting pan with parchment paper.

2 Put the figs and vinegar in a small saucepan over medium heat. Bring to a simmer. Cook for 1 minute. Remove the pan from the heat. Allow to stand for 10 minutes or until the liquid is absorbed.

3 Meanwhile, heat 1 tablespoon of the olive oil in a large skillet over medium heat. Cook the bread crumbs, stirring, for 5 minutes or until golden. Transfer to a small bowl. Wipe the pan clean with paper towels.

4 Heat another tablespoon of the olive oil in the same skillet over medium heat. Cook the onion, stirring, for 5 minutes or until soft. Add the garlic, lemon zest, and the 2 tablespoons finely chopped rosemary. Cook, stirring, for 1 minute or until fragrant. Remove the skillet from the heat. Stir in the parsley, bread crumbs, pine nuts, soaked fig mixture, and lemon juice. Season with salt and pepper to taste.

5 Arrange the sardines, in a single layer, in the lined roasting pan. Place a heaped tablespoon of the stuffing mixture inside each sardine. Fold the sardines over to enclose the filling. Top with any remaining stuffing mixture and the 2 tablespoons extra rosemary leaves. Drizzle with 1 tablespoon of the olive oil. Season with salt and pepper to taste. Bake the sardines in the oven for 15 minutes or until just cooked.

6 Meanwhile, brush the fennel and radicchio with the remaining olive oil. Season with salt and pepper to taste. Cook the fennel on a heated grill plate (or ridged cast-iron grill pan) over medium heat for 2 minutes on each side or until lightly charred. Transfer to a platter. Cook the radicchio wedges on the same grill plate for 1 minute on each side or until lightly charred and tender. Drizzle both with 1 tablespoon of the vincotto. Sprinkle with the reserved fennel fronds.

7 Drizzle the sardines with the remaining 1 tablespoon vincotto. Serve with the grilled fennel and radicchio, and lemon wedges for squeezing over.

Squid fattoush

PESCATARIAN | PREP + COOK TIME **50 MINUTES + REFRIGERATION** | SERVES **4**

Fattoush is a mainstay in Lebanon and Syria, and is a great way to serve toasted flatbread with fresh seasonal herbs, tomatoes, and cucumbers with zingy juices. Squid gives it some extra oomph. Serve with muhammara, a tangy roasted red pepper sauce (see page 186).

1½ tsp cumin seeds

1 tsp ground coriander

2 garlic cloves, crushed

½ tsp chili pepper flakes

¼ tsp ground sumac

¼ cup (60ml) extra virgin olive oil

2 tbsp lemon juice

1½ lbs (700g) squid hoods and tentacles

8oz (225g) baby cucumbers

1 cup (20g) flat-leaf parsley leaves

1 cup (20g) mint leaves

2 whole-wheat pita breads (160g), split in half horizontally (see tips)

8oz (225g) cherry tomatoes

salt and freshly ground black pepper

muhammara (see page 186), to serve

1 In a small skillet over medium heat, toast the cumin seeds and ground coriander, stirring, for 2 minutes or until fragrant. Transfer the spices to a medium bowl. Stir in the garlic, chili pepper flakes, sumac, olive oil, and lemon juice until combined.

2 Rinse the squid hoods and tentacles thoroughly under cold running water. Pat dry with paper towels. Place a cook's knife flat inside one of the squid hoods. Using a second knife, slice the squid crosswise at ½in intervals (as if you're cutting it into rings). The inserted knife will prevent you from cutting all the way through the squid. Repeat with the remaining squid. Add the squid hoods and tentacles to the spice mixture in the bowl. Toss to coat. Refrigerate for 2 hours.

3 Meanwhile, thinly slice the cucumbers into ribbons. Combine the cucumbers, parsley, and mint in a bowl.

4 Heat a ridged grill pan or barbeque. Grill the pita bread until toasted on both sides. Remove from the heat. Cook the squid hoods and tentacles until the squid is just cooked through and grill marks appear. Season with salt and pepper to taste.

5 Break the toasted pita bread into large pieces. Arrange the pita bread, squid, and tomatoes on a platter with the cucumber-herb salad. Serve with the muhammara for spooning over.

TIPS

- Ask your fishmonger to clean the squid hoods for you, reserving the tentacles.
- If it's difficult to split open the pita breads, microwave on HIGH (100%) for 10 seconds. The steam created from heating usually makes it easier to split open the bread.

Turkey keftas with date and barley pilaf

PREP + COOK TIME **1 HOUR 25 MINUTES + REFRIGERATION** | SERVES **4**

Keftas are a mainstay across Middle Eastern cuisine, and come in all shapes and sizes. This is especially so in Turkey, where they are a sort of art form and an especially popular street food. Using ground turkey instead of lamb adds freshness and lightness to these keftas.

1 lb (450g) ground turkey

1/2 cup (35g) fresh bread crumbs
(use day-old bread)

3 green onions, thinly sliced

2 garlic cloves, crushed

1/2 tsp allspice

1 tsp ground coriander

1/4 tsp chili powder

2 tbsp extra virgin olive oil

Greek yogurt, to serve

date and barley pilaf

2 tbsp extra virgin olive oil

1/4 cup (80g) finely chopped onion

2 garlic cloves, crushed

1 tbsp finely grated orange zest

1 tsp each of ground cinnamon, ground cumin,
and ground coriander

1 1/2 cups (300g) pearl barley

3 cups (750ml) chicken stock

2 tbsp chopped soft fresh dates such as Medjool

2 cups (100g) baby spinach leaves

salt and freshly ground black pepper

TIPS

- Use ground chicken instead of turkey, if you like.
- If using bamboo skewers, soak them in water for about 30 minutes before you start the recipe.
- The keftas can be made a day ahead. Store covered, in the fridge, until needed.

1   Combine the turkey, bread crumbs, green onions, garlic, allspice, coriander, and chili powder in a large bowl. Roll 2 tablespoons each of the mixture into 12 long oval shapes. Place the keftas on a baking sheet lined with parchment paper. Refrigerate for 1 hour.

2   To make the date and barley pilaf, heat the olive oil in a large saucepan over medium heat. Cook the onion and garlic for 5 minutes or until soft. Stir in the orange zest, cinnamon, cumin, and coriander. Cook for 2 minutes until fragrant. Add the pearl barley. Stir to coat. Pour in the stock. Bring to a boil, then reduce the heat to low. Cook, covered, for 30 minutes or until tender. Remove from the heat. Allow to stand, covered, for 10 minutes. Stir in the dates and spinach. Season with salt and pepper to taste.

3   Meanwhile, preheat a ridged cast-iron grill pan (or barbeque) to medium-high heat. Insert a metal or bamboo skewer into each of the keftas. Brush the keftas well with the olive oil. Cook, turning occasionally, for 8 minutes or until cooked through.

4   Serve the keftas accompanied by the date and barley pilaf, with yogurt for dolloping over the top.

Chargrilled chicken with fig and olive sauce

PREP + COOK TIME **55 MINUTES + RESTING & REFRIGERATION** | SERVES **4**

Very popular across the Middle East, dried fruit is often served at the end of the meal for dessert or offered to guests as a hospitable gesture, as well as being used to add depth to a variety of dishes. In this recipe, sweet, caramelized dried figs enhance the sauce.

3.5 lb (1.6kg) whole roasting chicken

4 garlic cloves, crushed

2 tbsp fresh rosemary leaves

1 tbsp finely grated orange zest

1/2 cup (125ml) orange juice

1/2 cup (125ml) extra virgin olive oil, divided

6 medium fresh figs (360g), quartered

5oz (142g) arugula

salt and freshly ground black pepper

lemon wedges, to serve

fig and olive sauce

1/3 cup (65g) coarsely chopped soft dried figs

1 tbsp Pedro Ximenez sherry or sweet dessert wine

1/2 cup (15g) coarsely chopped flat-leaf parsley

1/3 cup (55g) pitted kalamata olives

8 anchovy fillets

2 tsp capers

2 small garlic cloves, crushed

2 tsp finely grated lemon zest

1/2 cup (125ml) extra virgin olive oil

2 tbsp red wine vinegar

2 tbsp lemon juice

1   To butterfly the chicken, using a sharp, heavy knife or poultry shears, cut down both sides of the chicken backbone. Discard the backbone. Turn the chicken skin-side up. Press down on the breastbone with the heel of your hand to flatten. Pat dry with paper towels. Place in a large baking dish.

2   Combine the garlic, rosemary, orange zest, and juice, and 1/4 cup (60ml) of the olive oil in a large bowl. Pour over the chicken; turn to coat in the marinade. Cover. Refrigerate for at least 3 hours or overnight.

3   Meanwhile, to make the fig and olive sauce, combine the figs and sherry in a small bowl. Set aside for 10 minutes. In a food processor, add the softened fig mixture with the parsley, olives, anchovies, capers, garlic, lemon zest, and olive oil. Process until finely chopped. Stir in the vinegar and lemon juice. Season with salt and pepper to taste.

4   Preheat a cast iron grill plate, plancha, or barbeque grill to medium-high heat. Drain the chicken, reserving the marinade. Rub the chicken with the remaining 1/4 cup (60ml) olive oil. Season with salt and pepper to taste. Grill the chicken for 5 minutes on each side until well browned. Transfer to an ovenproof dish. Drizzle with the reserved marinade. Continue cooking the chicken with indirect heat for 30 minutes or until cooked through. Allow to rest for 10 minutes.

5   Serve the chicken with the combined figs and arugula, accompanied by the fig and olive sauce and lemon wedges for squeezing over.

TIPS

- The sauce can be made up to 3 days ahead. It will keep for up to 1 month in the fridge.
- You will need to start this recipe a day ahead. To save time, ask your butcher to butterfly the chicken.

Harissa tomato shrimp with feta cheese

PESCATARIAN | PREP + COOK TIME **25 MINUTES** | SERVES **4**

This is a contemporary twist on classic Middle Eastern flavors such as garlic, chili, and baharat. In Turkey, shrimp are often served in a tomato-based sauce, and the wine used here replaces Turkey's signature drink raki, distilled using grapes and flavored with anise.

1 tbsp extra virgin olive oil, plus extra 2 tsp

1/2 cup (150g) thinly sliced onion

2 garlic cloves, thinly sliced

1/4 cup (60ml) dry white wine

12oz large raw shrimp, peeled and deveined, with tails intact

2 tsp harissa (see page 186)

1 tsp baharat

1 x 14.5oz can (411g) diced tomatoes

1 tsp sugar

2 cups (400g) wholegrain couscous

4oz (110g) feta cheese, crumbled

curly endive, to serve

1   Preheat the broiler to high heat.

2   Heat the 1 tablespoon olive oil in a large, deep ovenproof skillet over medium heat. Cook the onion and garlic for 5 minutes or until tender. Add the wine. Cook over high heat for 30 seconds. Add the shrimp, harissa, and baharat. Cook, stirring occasionally, for 2 minutes. Add the tomatoes and sugar. Reduce the heat to low. Cook for 3 minutes or until the shrimp are just cooked. Season with salt and pepper to taste.

3   Meanwhile, put the couscous and 2 cups (500ml) boiling water in a large bowl. Cover with plastic wrap. Allow to stand for 5 minutes or until the water is absorbed. Fluff the couscous with a fork.

4   Scatter the feta cheese over the shrimp. Drizzle with the extra 2 teaspoons olive oil. Place the pan under the broiler for 2 minutes or until the feta cheese is golden. Serve the shrimp with the couscous and endive.

TIPS

- To adjust the spice, you can replace 1 teaspoon of the harissa with 1 teaspoon cumin seeds.
- An earthy, all-purpose spice mix, baharat is similar to garam masala in purpose and use. It is available from supermarkets, Middle Eastern grocers, and online. Lebanese or Syrian baharat is also known as seven-spice, after its characteristic composition, and has a sweeter, more mellow flavor than other variations found throughout the Middle East.
- This recipe is best made close to serving.

Chicken shawarma with crisp vegetables and yogurt sauce

PREP + COOK TIME **40 MINUTES + STANDING** | SERVES **4**

Shawarma is an Arab dish consisting of tender, succulent marinated meat shredded or cut into thin slices. A very popular street food, it is typically roasted on a spit, before being sliced or shaved, and served wrapped in flatbread. This is a lighter version with a crisp, fresh salad.

3 crushed garlic cloves, divided

2 tsp baharat (see tips)

2 tsp ground sumac, plus extra, to sprinkle

1 tbsp extra virgin olive oil

3 small lemons (195g), zest finely grated, then juiced

1 lb (500g) boneless, skinless chicken breasts

1/2 cup (140g) yogurt

1 wholegrain pita bread

1/4 cup (80g) thinly sliced red onion

1/2 cup (140g) thinly sliced red radishes

3 cucumbers (390g), thinly sliced

1 cup (30g) coarsely chopped mint leaves

1 cup (30g) coarsely chopped flat-leaf parsley leaves

2 x 1 lb heads (1 kg) iceberg lettuce, cored, leaves separated

freshly ground black pepper

TIPS

• Baharat is a warm and sweet aromatic spice blend typically made with a combination drawn from ground black peppercorns, coriander, cumin, allspice, cardamom, cinnamon, cloves, paprika, nutmeg. Specialties vary from region to region. It is available from supermarkets and Middle Eastern grocers, or make your own with the listed spices.

• If you have one, use a mandoline or V-slicer to shave the onion and radish very thinly.

1 Preheat the oven to 425°F. Line two baking sheets with parchment paper.

2 Combine two of the crushed garlic cloves, the baharat, the 2 teaspoons sumac, olive oil, 1 tablespoon of the lemon juice, and half of the lemon zest in a medium bowl. Add the chicken. Toss to coat. Allow to stand for 10 minutes.

3 To make the yogurt sauce, put the yogurt, remaining crushed garlic, remaining lemon zest, and 1 tablespoon of the lemon juice in a small bowl; whisk to combine. Season with pepper to taste.

4 Slice the pita bread open lengthwise. Put the chicken and its marinade on one lined sheet and the flatbread on the second sheet. Bake the pita for 8 minutes or until golden and crisp. Allow to cool. Bake the chicken for 15 minutes or until golden and cooked through. Allow the chicken to rest for 5 minutes. Thinly slice; toss in the cooking juices. Crumble the pita into small pieces.

5 Meanwhile, combine the onion, radishes, cucumbers, and remaining lemon juice in a bowl. Season with pepper to taste. Allow to stand for 15 minutes to lightly pickle the vegetables. Drain. Add the mint and parsley. Toss to combine.

6 Divide the lettuce leaves among four serving plates. Top with the chicken mixture, yogurt sauce, pickled vegetables and herbs, and crumbled pita.

Grilled calamari with oregano dressing and white bean purée

PESCATARIAN | PREP + COOK TIME 55 MINUTES + OVERNIGHT SOAKING | SERVES 4

Fresh herbs are integral to Middle Eastern cooking. They impart flavor and add freshness to meats, vegetables, pickles, and dips. In this recipe, the mildly earthy, peppery flavor of parsley is paired with earthier fresh oregano to create a sauce that doubles as a marinade.

You will need to start this recipe a day ahead

2 cups (400g) dried cannellini beans

2 tbsp extra virgin olive oil

1 cup (300g) chopped red onions

3 garlic cloves, crushed

4 cups (1 liter) vegetable stock

1/4 cup (60ml) fresh lemon juice

2 lbs (1kg) calamari hoods, thawed if frozen

salt and freshly ground black pepper

lemon wedges, to serve

oregano dressing

1 cup (40g) finely chopped flat-leaf parsley leaves

1/2 cup (15g) finely chopped oregano leaves

2 green onions, thinly sliced

2 tbsp baby capers

1 long red chile, seeded, finely chopped

1/4 cup (60ml) sherry vinegar

1/2 cup (125ml) extra virgin olive oil

TIPS

- The oregano dressing makes 1 cup (250ml) and can be made a day ahead. Store, covered, in the fridge.
- You can get your fishmonger to clean and prepare the calamari for you, if you like.

1 The day before cooking, put the cannellini beans in a large bowl. Cover with water and set aside to soak overnight. Drain.

2 The next day, heat the olive oil in a large saucepan over medium heat. Cook the onions and garlic, stirring occasionally, for 5 minutes. Add the drained beans and vegetable stock. Cover the pan; bring to a boil. Reduce the heat; simmer, covered, for 40 minutes. Drain the beans, reserving the cooking liquid. Process the beans, lemon juice, and enough of the reserved cooking liquid to form a thick, smooth purée. Season with salt and pepper to taste. Return to the pan. Cover to keep warm.

3 Wash the hoods and tentacles thoroughly. Pat dry with paper towels. Place a cook's knife flat inside one of the calamari hoods. Using a second knife, slice the calamari crosswise at 1/2-in intervals (as if you're cutting into rings). The knife will prevent you from cutting all the way through the calamari. Repeat with the remaining calamari.

4 To make the oregano dressing, combine the ingredients in a medium bowl. Season with salt and pepper to taste.

5 Preheat a ridged cast iron grill plate or barbecue grill to high heat. Put the calamari tubes and tentacles in a medium bowl. Add 1/4 cup (60ml) of the oregano dressing. Combine. Season with salt and pepper. Cook the calamari, in batches, for 1 minute on each side or until charred and cooked through.

6 Serve the calamari with the bean purée and oregano dressing.

Mint lamb skewers with garlic beans and yogurt sauce

PREP + COOK TIME **45 MINUTES** | SERVES **4**

Yogurt-based dipping sauces are spread right across the Middle East and Mediterranean, from the classic tzatziki of Greece and cacik of Turkey to the refreshing Lebanese sauce used in this recipe. They add freshness and acidity to grilled and roasted meats of all kinds.

$^1/_2$ cup (12g) firmly packed mint leaves

2 garlic cloves, quartered

$^1/_2$ tsp cracked black pepper

1 tbsp extra virgin olive oil

1 lb (550g) lamb loin or lamb neck, trimmed, cut into 8 long pieces

garlic beans

$^3/_4$ lb (400g) green beans, trimmed

2 tbsp extra virgin olive oil

1 garlic clove, thinly sliced

2 tbsp pine nuts, toasted

Lebanese yogurt sauce (khiyar bi laban)

1 large cucumber (130g)

1 garlic clove, crushed

1 cup (280g) Greek yogurt

2 tbsp lemon juice

salt and freshly ground black pepper

1 Using a mortar and pestle, pound the mint, garlic, and pepper until the mixture resembles a thick paste. Stir in the olive oil.

2 Thread the lamb onto 8 x 10in metal skewers. Put the lamb skewers in a shallow glass or ceramic dish; add the mint mixture. Turn the skewers to coat in the mixture.

3 To make the garlic beans, boil, steam, or microwave the green beans until just tender. Drain. Refresh in a large bowl of iced water. Drain again, then halve lengthwise. Place in a large bowl. Put the oil and garlic in a small skillet over low heat. Cook until the garlic is golden. Add the pine nuts. Stir until lightly golden. Drizzle the mixture over the beans.

4 To make the yogurt dressing, halve the cucumber lengthwise. Remove and discard any seeds (see tips). Coarsely grate the flesh (including the skin). Drain the grated cucumber in a sieve, pressing down lightly with a spoon, to remove any excess liquid. Transfer the cucumber to a medium bowl. Add the garlic, yogurt, and lemon juice. Stir to combine. Season with salt and pepper to taste.

5 Preheat a cast-iron ridged grill plate or barbecue grill to medium-high heat. Cook the lamb skewers, turning occasionally, for 10 minutes for medium, or until cooked as desired.

6 Serve the lamb with the garlic beans and yogurt dressing.

TIPS

- Run a teaspoon down the center of the cucumber to remove any seeds.
- If you use bamboo skewers, soak them in boiling water for 10 minutes before using, to prevent them from burning during cooking.

Vine-wrapped fish with yogurt tartare sauce and sweet potato wedges

PESCATARIAN | PREP + COOK TIME **45 MINUTES** | SERVES **4**

Grape vine leaves are much used in Middle Eastern and Mediterranean food, and this recipe is a clever contemporary twist on traditional fish 'n' chips with tartare sauce. Its sweet, sour, and salty elements meld into a glorious combination of flavor and texture.

2 lbs (1kg) orange sweet potatoes, unpeeled, cut into wedges

6 sprigs of oregano

1/4 cup (60ml) extra virgin olive oil, divided

2 1/2 lbs (1kg) whiting, cod, or grouper, cleaned

8 medium preserved vine leaves, rinsed

2 tbsp fresh dill sprigs

salt and freshly ground black pepper

lemon wedges, to serve

yogurt tartare sauce

1 cup (280g) Greek yogurt

2 tbsp capers, chopped

6 cornichons (90g), chopped

1 tbsp white balsamic vinegar

1/4 cup (10g) finely chopped dill

1   Preheat the oven to 400°F. Line a baking sheet with parchment paper.

2   Put the sweet potato and oregano on the parchment-lined sheet. Drizzle with 1 tablespoon of the olive oil. Season with salt and pepper to taste, then toss to coat. Roast for 30 minutes or until golden and tender.

3   Meanwhile, to make the yogurt tartare sauce, combine the ingredients in a medium bowl. Season with salt and pepper to taste.

4   Preheat a large non-stick saute pan to medium heat. Wrap each fish in a vine leaf; drizzle with the remaining olive oil. Cook the fish, in batches, for 3 minutes on each side or until cooked through.

5   Serve the fish and sweet potato wedges topped with the dill sprigs, accompanied by the yogurt tartare sauce for spooning on top and lemon wedges for squeezing over.

TIPS

• Preserved vine leaves are available from Middle Eastern and Greek grocers and delicatessens, as well as at some supermarkets and online.

• In season, you can also use 8 whole, cleaned fresh sardines, if you'd like.

Shish tawook with cucumber yogurt

PREP + COOK TIME **40 MINUTES** | SERVES **4**

Shish kebabs or shashlik are extremely popular across the Middle East and into the Caucasus and Central Asia. In this version, chicken is marinated in lemon juice and yogurt before being threaded onto skewers and grilled, giving the meat a wonderful smoky flavor and succulence.

1/3 cup (80ml) extra virgin olive oil, divided

1/3 cup (80ml) lemon juice, divided

1/2 cup (180g) Greek yogurt

4 garlic cloves, crushed

1/2 tsp ground paprika

1/2 tsp ground cinnamon

1/4 cup (12g) chopped mint leaves

2 tsp finely grated lemon zest

1 3/4 lb (800g) chicken thigh fillets, cut into 1in cubes

salt and freshly ground black pepper

cucumber yogurt

1 cup (280g) Greek yogurt

4oz (130g) baby cucumbers, coarsely grated, drained

1 green onion, thinly sliced

1/3 cup (7g) mint leaves, chopped

2 tbsp lemon juice

sprigs of fresh dill, to garnish

to serve

pita bread

curly endive

sliced red onion

1 Combine half of the olive oil and half of the lemon juice with the yogurt, paprika, cinnamon, mint, lemon zest, and chicken in a large bowl. Season with salt and pepper to taste. Refrigerate for at least 30 minutes or longer if possible, to allow the flavors to combine.

2 To make the cucumber yogurt, combine the yogurt, cucumber, green onion, mint, and the 2 tablespoons lemon juice in a bowl. Season with salt and pepper to taste. Garnish with dill sprigs.

3 Preheat a ridged cast-iron grill pan or barbeque grill to high heat. Thread the chicken onto metal skewers. Grill the chicken, turning occasionally, for 10 minutes or until nicely charred all over and just cooked through. Transfer the skewers to a plate. Cover with foil to keep warm.

4 Whisk together the remaining olive oil and lemon juice. Serve the chicken skewers with the cucumber yogurt, pita bread, curly endive, and red onion, with the oil-lemon dressing drizzled over the top.

Baharat chicken wraps with pickled radish and garlic sauce

PREP + COOK TIME **1 HOUR 15 MINUTES** | SERVES **6**

Baharat is the Arabic word for "spice" and refers to the complex spice blend that is used to add a real depth of flavor to many Middle Eastern dishes. It usually includes black pepper, cumin, coriander, cloves, cardamom, paprika, cinnamon, and nutmeg—variations abound and not only do individual ratios vary, but the makeup of actual spices used can do so as well.

2 tbsp baharat

1/4 cup (70g) Dijon mustard

2 tsp finely grated lemon zest

2 tbsp lemon juice

8 chicken thighs (1.6kg)

2 tbsp white wine vinegar

2 tsp sea salt flakes

2 tsp sugar

1 1/2 cups (450g) thinly shaved radishes

6 large pita flatbreads, cut in half

2 romaine hearts (130g), cut into wedges

4 baby cucumbers (120g), cut into ribbons

salt and freshly ground black pepper

garlic sauce

4 garlic cloves, unpeeled

1 cup (280g) Greek yogurt

2 tsp baharat

1 tsp finely grated lemon zest

1 tbsp lemon juice

1/3 cup (15g) finely chopped mint leaves

1 Preheat the oven to 350°F.

2 Toast the baharat in a small skillet over low heat for 2 minutes or until fragrant.

3 Combine the baharat, mustard, lemon zest, and lemon juice in a large bowl. Season with salt and pepper to taste. Add the chicken. Turn to coat well. Transfer to a large roasting pan or ovenproof baking dish. Roast in the oven, covered, for 1 hour or until very tender. Allow to cool slightly. Shred or chop the chicken, discarding any skin and bones. Combine the chicken with enough of the cooking juices to moisten. Season with salt and pepper to taste.

4 Meanwhile, to make the garlic sauce, roast the garlic on a small baking sheet or in a shallow baking dish. Bake in the oven with the chicken for 15 minutes or until tender. Squeeze the garlic from the skins into a small bowl. Mash with a fork. Add the yogurt, baharat, lemon zest and juice, and mint. Season with salt and pepper to taste.

5 Stir together the vinegar, salt, and sugar in a medium bowl until the sugar dissolves. Add the radishes. Set aside to lightly pickle. Season with pepper to taste.

6 To serve, spread the warmed flatbread with the garlic sauce. Top with the lettuce, shredded chicken, pickled radish, and cucumbers, ready to roll up into wraps for eating.

Saffron and lemon chicken with crispy shallot rice

PREP + COOK TIME **1 HOUR 15 MINUTES** | SERVES **4**

With its echoes of a classic Persian pilaf, this impressive-looking dish is easy to prepare. You can barbecue the chicken instead of roasting it, if you like, which adds a lovely smoky flavor. Simply serve with fresh lemon, instead of placing the slices over the chicken during cooking.

$^1/_2$ tsp saffron threads

3 lemons (420g)

2 tbsp extra virgin olive oil

4 garlic cloves, crushed

5 lb whole roasting chicken, butterflied or spatchcocked (see tip)

8oz (260g) fresh spinach leaves

salt and freshly ground black pepper

crispy onion rice

1 cup (200g) basmati rice

$^1/_3$ cup (80ml) extra virgin olive oil

$^3/_4$ cup (200g) thinly sliced shallot (see tip)

1 15.5 oz can (439g) can chickpeas, drained, rinsed

$^1/_4$ cup (80g) chopped fresh dates such as Medjool

$^1/_2$ cup (20g) firmly packed chopped flat-leaf parsley

$^1/_2$ cup (50g) flaked almonds, toasted

TIPS

- Ask your butcher to butterfly the chicken.
- Use a mandoline or V-slicer to cut the shallots into very thin slices. You will need to get a good color on the shallots, but be careful not to overcook them or they will become bitter.

1 Preheat the oven to 400°F. Line an ovenproof casserole or baking dish with parchment paper. Combine the saffron and 2 teaspoons boiling water in a small cup. Set aside for 10 minutes.

2 Cut 1 of the lemons into $^1/_4$-in slices; reserve. Finely grate the zest of the remaining 2 lemons, then juice. You will need 1 tablespoon lemon zest and $^1/_4$ cup (60ml) lemon juice.

3 Combine the olive oil, saffron and its soaking liquid, garlic, and lemon zest and juice in a small bowl. Season well with salt and pepper. Put the chicken in the lined baking dish. Brush the saffron mixture all over the chicken, then cover with the reserved lemon slices. Roast the chicken for 1 hour or until browned and cooked through. Set aside to rest.

4 Meanwhile, to make the crispy onion rice, rinse the rice in a sieve under cold running water until the water runs clear. Put the rice and 1$^1/_2$ cups (375ml) water in a medium saucepan over high heat. Bring to a boil. Reduce the heat to low. Simmer, covered, for 12 minutes. Remove from the heat. Allow to stand, covered, for 10 minutes. Fluff with a fork.

5 While the rice is cooking, heat the olive oil in a medium frying pan over medium-high heat. Cook the onions, stirring, for 7 minutes or until browned and crisp. Transfer to a plate lined with paper towels. Cook the chickpeas in the same pan, stirring, for 5 minutes or until lightly browned. Put the rice and chickpeas in a large bowl with the dates and parsley. Season with salt and pepper to taste. Toss to combine. Add the onions and the almonds. Stir gently to combine.

6 Heat a skillet over medium-high heat. Add the spinach and 2 tablespoons water. Cook, stirring, for 1 minute or until just wilted. Season with salt and pepper to taste.

7 Cut the chicken into serving pieces. Serve with the crispy rice and spinach, drizzled with the pan juices.

Baked whole snapper with lemony tahini

PESCATARIAN | PREP + COOK TIME **45 MINUTES** | SERVES **4**

Snapper is one of the few white fish varieties that will hold up to the heat of the oven and bake really well, holding its shape while still remaining tender and flaky. The rice mixture used here also helps to keep the fish whole and moist for eating.

1 package (250g) precooked brown and wild rice

1/4 cup (40g) dried currants

1/2 cup (15g) finely chopped flat-leaf parsley, plus extra leaves, to serve

1 garlic clove, crushed

2 tsp finely grated lemon zest

2 tbsp extra virgin olive oil, divided

1/2 cup (125ml) lemon juice

5 lbs whole snapper (2–3 fish), cleaned

1 1/2 tbsp ras el hanout

1/2 cup (140g) tahini

salt and freshly ground black pepper

lemon wedges, to serve

1 Preheat the oven to 400°F. Line 2 large baking sheets with parchment paper.

2 Heat the rice according to the package directions.

3 Put the rice in a medium bowl with the currants, 1/3 cup (10g) of the parsley, the garlic, lemon zest, 1 tablespoon of the olive oil, and 2 tablespoons of the lemon juice. Season with salt and pepper to taste, then toss gently to combine. Set aside.

4 Using a sharp knife, make 2 shallow diagonal cuts in the thickest part of the snapper flesh on both sides of the fish. Drizzle the fish with the remaining olive oil. Rub both sides with the ras el hanout. Season with salt and pepper to taste. Fill the cavity of each fish with the rice mixture. Place the fish on the lined sheets.

5 Bake in the oven for 35 minutes or until the fish is just cooked.

6 Meanwhile, in a food processor, combine the tahini and 1/4 cup (60ml) water with the remaining chopped parsley and the remaining lemon juice until smooth. Season with salt and pepper to taste.

7 Serve the fish with the lemony tahini, extra parsley leaves, and lemon wedges for squeezing over.

TIP

Serve the fish with roasted vegetables or a fresh salad for a complete meal.

Roast herbed lamb with walnut salad

PREP + COOK TIME **1 HOUR** | SERVES **6**

Succulent roast lamb gets the full Middle Eastern treatment with a combination of both fresh and dried herbs used to make a fragrant chermoula topping that packs a flavor punch. The accompanying walnut salad lifts this further with its crunch and piquant freshness.

1 tbsp extra virgin olive oil

3¹/₂ lbs (1.5kg) boneless leg of lamb, trimmed and butterflied

salt and freshly ground black pepper

chermoula topping

1 cup (20g) flat-leaf parsley leaves

1 cup (30g) cilantro leaves

4 garlic cloves, crushed

1 long green chile, chopped

3 tsp ground cumin

2 tsp ground coriander

2 tsp sweet paprika

¹/₃ cup (80ml) extra virgin olive oil

¹/₃ cup (80ml) lemon juice

walnut salad

1 cup (115g) walnuts, roasted, coarsely chopped

1¹/₄ cup (80g), finely chopped red onion

12 oz (400g) plum tomatoes, halved

¹/₃ cup (20g) finely chopped cilantro

¹/₄ cup (60ml) extra virgin olive oil

1 tbsp pomegranate molasses

1 Preheat the oven to 400°F.

2 To make the chermoula topping, in a food processor, combine the ingredients and pulse until smooth. Season with salt and pepper to taste. Set aside.

3 Heat the olive oil in an oven proof roasting pan over high heat. Cook the lamb for 3 minutes on each side or until well browned. Season with salt and pepper to taste. Remove the pan from the heat. Pour the chermoula over the lamb, coating well. Roast in the oven for 30 minutes for medium, or until the lamb is cooked to your liking. Let rest for 10 minutes.

4 Meanwhile, to make the walnut salad, combine the ingredients in a medium bowl. Season with salt and pepper to taste.

5 Serve the sliced lamb with pan juices and the walnut salad.

TIP

To ensure even cooking, choose a piece of lamb with an even thickness.

Roast beef sirloin with charred zucchini and smoky tahini

PREP + COOK TIME **1 HOUR 10 MINUTES** | SERVES **6**

The combination of smoked paprika and harissa imparts a wonderful, deep nuanced flavor to classic roast beef. Making your own spice rub also allows you to choose the freshest, most fragrant spices and seeds so that their individual flavors don't dull and flatten.

1/4 cup (60ml) extra virgin olive oil, divided

3 1/2 lbs (1.5kg) beef top sirloin roast, trimmed, tied with string at 2-in intervals

2 lbs zucchini (900g), halved lengthwise

salt and freshly ground black pepper

spice mix

3 tsp coriander seeds

2 tsp cumin seeds

2 tsp fennel seeds

1 tbsp smoked paprika

1 tsp harissa spice blend

1 tbsp white sesame seeds

smoky tahini

1/4 cup (70g) tahini

1/3 cup (80ml) lemon juice

1 garlic clove, crushed

1 tsp smoked paprika

2oz (60g) feta cheese

1 Preheat the oven to 400°F.

2 To make the spice mix, toast the coriander, cumin, and fennel seeds in a small frying pan over medium heat for 2 minutes or until fragrant. Transfer to a spice grinder or use a mortar and pestle. Blend or pound until coarse. Combine the coarsely ground seeds with the paprika, harissa, and sesame seeds in a small bowl.

3 Heat 1 tablespoon of the olive oil in a large roasting pan. Cook the beef, turning, for 5 minutes or until browned all over. Rub half of the spice mix all over the beef. Season with salt and pepper to taste. Transfer the pan to the oven. Roast for 25 minutes for medium-rare. Allow to rest, covered, for 10 minutes.

4 Meanwhile, to make the smoky tahini, combine the ingredients in a food processor until smooth. Season with salt and pepper to taste.

5 Preheat a ridged cast iron grill pan to high heat. Combine the remaining olive oil and the remaining spice mix in a large bowl. Add the zucchini, turning to coat. Grill the zucchini for 5 minutes on each side or until well charred and tender.

6 Thinly slice the beef. Serve with the pan juices, charred zucchini, and smoky tahini.

Baked rainbow trout with radish salad and citrus dressing

PESCATARIAN | PREP + COOK TIME **35 MINUTES** | SERVES **4**

Orange and bay leaf aren't often used when cooking trout, as they are usually considered too overpowering for delicate fish. But in reality the strong, distinct flavors of orange and bay hold up really well against the fatty oils and robust flesh of rainbow trout.

3¹/₂ lbs (1.8kg) rainbow trout, cleaned and scaled

2 oranges (360g)

4 sprigs of fresh bay leaf

¹/₂ cup (125ml) extra virgin olive oil, divided

1 cup (250ml) chicken stock

1 cup (200g) wholegrain couscous

1 tbsp lemon juice

³/₄ cup (200g) thinly sliced watermelon radishes

1 baby fennel bulb (130g),
cut into wedges, fronds reserved

¹/₂ cup (15g) firmly packed mint leaves

¹/₂ cup (15g) firmly packed flat-leaf parsley leaves

salt and freshly ground black pepper

1   Preheat the oven to 475°F. Line 2 large baking sheets with parchment paper.

2   Place the fish on the lined sheets. Slice 1 of the oranges. Fill each fish cavity with the orange slices and sprigs of bay leaf. Season with salt and pepper to taste, then drizzle with 1 tablespoon of the olive oil. Bake for 12 minutes or until just cooked through, turning over halfway through the cooking time.

3   Meanwhile, put the chicken stock in a small saucepan. Bring to a boil. Add the couscous; remove from the heat. Allow to stand, covered, for 5 minutes. Stir with a fork to fluff up the grains. Season with salt and pepper to taste.

4   To make the citrus dressing, finely grate the zest from the remaining orange, then juice the orange. Put the remaining olive oil, orange zest, orange juice, and lemon juice in a screw-top jar with a tight-fitting lid; shake well. Season with salt and pepper to taste.

5   Combine the radishes, fennel wedges, mint, parsley, and half of the dressing in a medium bowl.

6   Serve the fish with the couscous and radish salad, topped with the reserved fennel fronds. Drizzle with more of the citrus dressing.

TIPS

- Whole salmon or any flaky white fish can be used in place of the trout; the cooking time will vary.
- For a gluten-free option, use quinoa instead of the couscous.
- Serve with a fresh Greek salad or a simple leaf salad dressed in olive oil and lemon juice, if you like.

Quinoa tabbouleh with lamb and sesame eggs

PREP + COOK TIME **35 MINUTES** | SERVES **4**

Tabbouleh is a quintessential part of most mezze platters. The parsley salad is traditionally made with bulgur wheat, but you can also find modern versions that use semolina or quinoa, such as this recipe. Tabbouleh is also a fantastic accompaniment to red or white meats, or falafel, especially when wrapped together in pita bread.

1 cup (200g) quinoa, rinsed

2 cups (500ml) vegetable stock

2 tbsp extra virgin olive oil, divided

1 garlic clove, crushed

1$^{1}/_{2}$ lbs (750g) rainbow chard, stems removed, leaves thinly sliced (see tip)

2 tbsp lemon juice

$^{3}/_{4}$ lb (400g) lamb loin

4 eggs, at room temperature

$^{3}/_{4}$ cup (30g) finely chopped flat-leaf parsley

2 tbsp white sesame seeds

2 tbsp black sesame seeds

1 tsp salt

freshly ground black pepper

1. Put the quinoa and vegetable stock in a large saucepan. Bring to a boil. Reduce the heat to low-medium. Simmer gently, covered, for 15 minutes or until most of the stock is absorbed. Remove from the heat. Allow to stand for 5 minutes.

2. Heat 1 tablespoon of the olive oil in a medium saucepan over medium heat. Cook the garlic, stirring, for 1 minute or until fragrant. Add the chard leaves. Stir until wilted. Add the cooked quinoa and lemon juice. Season with salt and pepper to taste.

3. Season the lamb with salt and pepper to taste. Heat the remaining olive oil in a heavy sauté pan over high heat. Cook the lamb for 4 minutes on each side, or until cooked to your liking. Transfer to a plate. Allow to rest for 5 minutes, then thickly slice.

4. Meanwhile, cook the eggs in a small saucepan of boiling water for 5 minutes for soft-boiled. Remove immediately and cool under cold running water for 30 seconds.

5. Combine the parsley, sesame seeds, and the 1 teaspoon salt in a small bowl. Peel the eggs. Roll in the parsley mixture.

6. Serve the quinoa tabbouleh topped with the sliced lamb and halved eggs.

TIP

Chop the chard stems and freeze for use in soups and stocks.

Banquet menu

Ideal for a relaxed lunch or unhurried entertaining, or even a weeknight meal, the dishes here work in tandem to form a wealth of vibrant tastes and textures. Simple to put together and even simpler to bring to the table, their success lies in choosing the best produce you can find and letting the ingredients shine while you enjoy the company and conversation of family and friends.

BANQUET RECIPES

SOUPS
AND STEWS

You will find everything here from simple but tasty soups and warming broths, to classic tagines from the Maghrebi tradition and rich, hearty braises of meat and seafood.

Turkish-style braised red mullet

PESCATARIAN | PREP + COOK TIME **50 MINUTES** | SERVES **4**

Adding sumac to dukkah imparts a zesty, lemonlike flavor to an otherwise warm and spicy condiment. While dukkah has Egyptian origins, braising the red mullet in a tomatoey sauce dominated by fresh, seasonal ingredients gives this dish a distinctly Turkish stamp.

4 red bell peppers, halved, seeded (see tips)

1/4 cup (60ml) extra virgin olive oil

2 red onions (340g), thinly sliced

4 garlic cloves, thinly sliced

1/2 tsp chili pepper flakes

2 tsp paprika

1 tsp granulated sugar

2 tbsp tomato paste

10oz (350g) cherry tomatoes, halved

1 x 28oz can (793g) crushed tomato

1 x 15.5oz (439g) can chickpeas, drained, rinsed

1/3 cup (10g) fresh oregano, divided

1¼ lb (640g) boneless red mullet fillets (see tip)

5oz (150g) feta cheese, crumbled

salt and freshly ground black pepper

grilled flatbread, to serve

almond and sumac dukkah

2 tbsp blanched almonds, roasted, coarsely chopped

2 tsp cumin seeds, lightly toasted

1 tsp finely grated lemon zest

1/2 tsp sumac

1 tbsp finely chopped flat-leaf parsley

1   Preheat the boiler to high. Arrange the peppers, skin-side up, on a large baking sheet lined with foil. Place under the hot boiler for 8 minutes or until the skin blisters and blackens. Place the peppers in a plastic zip top bag or a bowl covered in plastic wrap. Let steam. When cool enough to handle, peel away the skin and discard. Cut the peppers in half lengthwise once again.

2   Meanwhile, heat the olive oil in a large, deep heavy-based sauté pan over medium heat. Cook the onion, stirring, for 8 minutes or until softened. Add the garlic, chili pepper flakes, paprika, sugar, and tomato paste. Cook, stirring, for 2 minutes or until fragrant. Add the fresh and canned tomatoes, chickpeas, and 1/4 cup (7g) of the oregano. Bring to a simmer over medium heat. Cook, covered, for 5 minutes. Stir in the grilled peppers. Season with salt and pepper to taste.

3   Next, season the fish with salt and pepper to taste. Add to the pan, making sure to spoon some of the sauce over the fish. Reduce the heat to low. Cook, covered, for 6 minutes or until the fish is just cooked through.

4   Meanwhile, to make the almond and sumac dukkah, combine the ingredients in a small bowl.

5   To serve, top the fish with crumbled feta cheese, the remaining oregano, and dukkah. Serve with the grilled bread for mopping up the juices.

TIP

▪ You can find pre-made dukkah in the spice aisle of your favorite gourmet or specialty grocery store.

▪ If you like, use your favorite firm white fish, such as ling, snapper, or whiting, in place of red mullet.

Spicy beans with crunchy croutons

PREP + COOK TIME **1 HOUR 20 MINUTES + OVERNIGHT SOAKING** | SERVES **6 (MAKES 7 CUPS)**

Cuisines across the Middle East and North Africa have a strong foundation in fresh vegetables and a variety of grains, legumes, and pulses. White bean stew, in all its variations, is one example. This is a meat-free version, with croutons replacing the traditional vermicelli rice.

You will need to start this recipe the day before

³/₄ lb (400g) dried white beans such as Great Northern or cannellini

10oz (350g) sourdough bread, torn into rough chunks

¹/₃ cup (80ml) extra virgin olive oil, divided

2 tbsp chopped thyme leaves

1 cup (300g) finely chopped onions

8 garlic cloves, thinly sliced

2 hot peppers, thinly sliced

1 tsp smoked paprika

¹/₄ cup (70g) tomato paste

1¹/₄ cup (660g) tomatoes, coarsely chopped

3 cups (750ml) vegetable stock

¹/₂ cup (45g) grated Parmesan cheese

salt and freshly ground black pepper

TIPS

- The recipe can be made 2 days ahead. Store the beans, covered, in the fridge. Store the croutons in an airtight container at room temperature. You can use any dried bean in this recipe such as haricot, butterbeans, kidney, or borlotti. Cooking times will vary slightly.
- If you do forget to soak your beans the day before, use this fast-soak method: Put the beans in a saucepan. Cover with water. Slowly bring to a boil. Boil for 5 minutes. Remove from the heat. Allow the beans to cool in the cooking liquid. Drain and rinse well before continuing from step 2.

1 Put the beans in a large bowl with enough cold water to cover. Let soak overnight.

2 The next day, drain the beans. Rinse well under cold running water. Put the beans in a medium saucepan with enough cold water to cover. Bring to a boil. Reduce the heat to low-medium. Simmer for 30 minutes or until the beans are almost tender. Drain.

3 Meanwhile, preheat the oven to 400°F. Combine the bread with half of the olive oil and 1 tablespoon of the chopped thyme on a large baking sheet. Toss gently to combine. Bake for 12 minutes or until golden and crisp. Set aside to cool.

4 Heat the remaining olive oil in a large saucepan over medium heat. Add the onions, garlic, peppers, and paprika. Cook, stirring, for 7 minutes or until the onion is golden. Add the tomato paste, tomatoes, the remaining 1 tablespoon chopped thyme, and the stock. Bring to a boil. Reduce the heat to medium. Simmer, covered, for 10 minutes or until the sauce thickens slightly. Add the beans. Simmer, covered, for a further 10 minutes, stirring occasionally. Remove the lid. Continue to simmer for 10 minutes or until the beans are tender and the sauce has again thickened slightly. Season with salt and pepper to taste.

5 Serve the spicy beans topped with the Parmesan cheese and scattered with the sourdough croutons.

Vegetable tagine with za'atar chickpeas

VEGETARIAN | PREP + COOK TIME **1 HOUR** | SERVES **4**

Although not made in the traditional earthenware pot, this tagine nonetheless marries the classic cooking technique of the Berber people of North Africa with the flavors of the Middle East to create a delicious and fragrant vegetarian meal.

2 tsp extra virgin olive oil

1 cup (300g) coarsely chopped onion

2 garlic cloves, crushed

1/2 lb (225g) eggplant, halved lengthwise

1 lb (500g) kabocha squash, peeled, cut into 1 inch pieces

2 tsp ground cumin

2 tsp ground coriander

2 tsp ground ginger

1/2 tsp ground cinnamon

1 x 14.5oz (411g) can diced tomatoes

2 cups (500ml) vegetable stock

3/4 lb (300g) small zucchini, trimmed, halved lengthwise

3/4 cup Greek yogurt

1/2 cup (20g) finely chopped flat-leaf parsley, plus extra leaves, to serve

salt and freshly ground black pepper

za'atar chickpeas

1 x 15.5oz (439g) can chickpeas, drained, rinsed

1 tbsp za'atar

2 tbsp extra virgin olive oil

1. To make the za'atar chickpeas, pat the chickpeas dry with paper towels. Put in a medium bowl, then toss with the za'atar. Heat the olive oil in a small frying pan over medium heat. Cook the chickpea mixture, stirring, for 10 minutes or until golden.

2. Meanwhile, to make the tagine, heat the olive oil in a large heavy-based saucepan over medium heat. Cook the onion and garlic, stirring, for 5 minutes. Add the eggplant and squash. Cook for 1 minute on each side or until the vegetables are lightly browned. Add the ground spices. Cook for 1 minute or until fragrant. Add the canned tomatoes, stock, and zucchini. Bring to a boil. Reduce the heat to low. Simmer, covered, for 15 minutes or until the vegetables are just tender.

3. Combine the yogurt and parsley in a small bowl. Season with salt and pepper to taste.

4. Serve the tagine topped with the yogurt mixture, za'atar chickpeas, and extra parsley leaves.

TIP

Instead of making the za'atar chickpeas, you could add the chickpeas to the tagine when adding the tomatoes in step 2.

Lamb and apricot tagine

PREP + COOK TIME **2 HOURS 20 MINUTES** | SERVES **6**

Dried fruits feature in various cuisines and among various peoples across the Middle East and into North Africa, with characteristic dishes often having long historical associations. This tagine, with its pairing of lamb and apricots, is evocative of Morocco and Tunisia.

2 tbsp extra virgin olive oil, divided

2¹/₄ lb (1kg) boneless lamb shoulder, trimmed, cut into 2 in pieces

¹/₂ cup (150g) thinly sliced onion

2 garlic cloves, crushed

1 tsp ground cumin

1 tsp ground coriander

1 tsp ground cinnamon

2 cups (500ml) beef stock

¹/₂ cup (75g) dried apricot halves

4oz (100g) spinach leaves

¹/₄ cup (40g) blanched almonds, toasted

salt and freshly ground black pepper

couscous, to serve

1 Heat 1 tablespoon of the olive oil in a large saucepan over medium-high heat. Cook the lamb, in batches, until well browned. Season with salt and pepper to taste. Remove from the pan.

2 Heat the remaining 1 tablespoon olive oil in the same pan over medium heat. Cook the onion and garlic, stirring, for 5 minutes or until the onion softens. Add the cumin, coriander, and cinnamon. Cook, stirring, for 1 minute or until fragrant.

3 Return the lamb to the pan with the stock. Bring to a boil. Reduce the heat. Simmer, covered, for 1 hour 40 minutes. Add the apricots. Simmer, covered, for a further 20 minutes or until the lamb is very tender. Stir in the spinach. Season with salt and pepper to taste.

4 To serve, top the tagine with the toasted almonds. Serve with couscous.

TIP

For something different, try chicken or beef instead of lamb, if you like. You will need to adjust the cooking time accordingly.

Haloumi and shrimp stuffed squid

PESCATARIAN | PREP + COOK TIME **1 HOUR 35 MINUTES** | SERVES **4**

Whether you know it as squid or as calamari, this seafood gem benefits from either very quick cooking or a slow braise, as in this Turkish-style stew. Instead of bulgur wheat to bind the filling, quinoa flakes are used for a flavorful twist and gluten-free friendly alternative.

1 lb (450g) uncooked shrimp, peeled, deveined, chopped

$^1/_2$ cup (40g) quinoa flakes

1 tsp finely grated lemon zest

8oz (225g) haloumi cheese, grated

$1^1/_4$ lb (630g) calamari or squid hoods, cleaned, tentacles removed

2 tbsp extra virgin olive oil, divided, plus extra, to drizzle

$^1/_4$ cup (80g) finely chopped onion

1 tsp smoked paprika

$^1/_2$ cup (125ml) dry white wine

1 x 28oz can (793g) crushed tomatoes

1 cup (250ml) vegetable stock

$^1/_2$ tsp dried pepper flakes

1 tsp light brown sugar

$^1/_3$ cup (10g) coarsely chopped flat-leaf parsley, plus extra, to serve

crusty bread and lemon wedges, to serve

1 Combine the shrimp, quinoa, lemon zest, and haloumi cheese in a large bowl. Finely chop the reserved squid tentacles. Stir into the shrimp mixture. Season with pepper to taste.

2 Spoon the stuffing mixture into the squid hoods. Secure the openings with toothpicks.

3 Heat 1 tablespoon of the olive oil in a deep, heavy-bottomed sauté pan over medium-high heat. Cook the squid, turning, for 8 minutes or until golden all over. Remove from the pan.

4 Heat the remaining 1 tablespoon olive oil in the same pan. Cook the onion, stirring, for 5 minutes or until softened. Add the paprika. Cook, stirring, for 30 seconds until fragrant. Pour in the wine. Simmer for 3 minutes or until almost evaporated. Stir in the tomatoes, stock, dried pepper flakes, and sugar. Bring to a boil. Return the squid to the pan. Reduce the heat to low. Cook, stirring and turning the squid occasionally, for 35 minutes or until the squid is tender. Stir in the $^1/_3$ cup (10g) coarsely chopped parsley.

5 Remove the squid from the sauce; discard the toothpicks. Cut the squid into thick slices on the diagonal.

6 To serve, place the stuffed squid on top of the sauce. Drizzle with extra olive oil and top with extra parsley. Serve with crusty bread and lemon wedges for squeezing over.

Cauliflower and pistachio soup with sumac roast cauliflower

VEGETARIAN | PREP + COOK TIME **1 HOUR 10 MINUTES** | SERVES **4**

Made from the dried, ground berries of the wild sumac shrub, sumac is tangy, zesty, and sour, adding a distinct lemony undertone to this soup. Used as a condiment and seasoning across the Middle East, it is one of the core ingredients in za'atar and in salads such as fattoush.

2 cups (300g) unsalted shelled pistachios, plus extra $1/4$ cup (35g), finely chopped

4 lbs (2kg) cauliflower heads

2 tbsp ghee, plus extra 1 tsp

$3/4$ cup (200g) coarsely chopped onion

3 garlic cloves, crushed

$3/4$ cup (200g) sliced leek

$1/2$ tsp ground cinnamon

2 tsp ground cumin

$5^1/2$ cups (1.4 liters) vegetable stock

2 tsp ground sumac

salt and freshly ground black pepper

flatbread, to serve

1 Preheat the oven to 400°F. Line a baking sheet with parchment paper.

2 Put the pistachios in a medium heatproof bowl; add enough boiling water to cover. Allow to stand for 20 minutes. Drain well. Wrap the pistachios in a clean dish towel; rub vigorously to remove the skins. Discard the skins.

3 Meanwhile, reserve the small cauliflower leaves and $1/4$ lb (100g) of small florets. Cut the remaining cauliflower into large florets.

4 Heat the 2 tablespoons ghee in a large saucepan over medium heat. Cook the onion, garlic, and leek, stirring, for 8 minutes or until softened. Add the cinnamon and cumin. Cook for 1 minute until fragrant. Next, add the large cauliflower florets, skinless pistachios, and stock. Bring to a boil. Reduce the heat. Simmer for 30 minutes or until the cauliflower is very tender. Season with salt and pepper to taste.

5 Meanwhile, combine the reserved small cauliflower florets and leaves, 1 teaspoon of the sumac, and the extra 1 teaspoon ghee on the lined baking sheet. Season with salt and pepper to taste. Bake for 20 minutes or until the cauliflower is golden and the edges are crisp.

6 Add the soup to a blender or food process and pulse until smooth. Ladle the soup into serving bowls. Top with the roasted cauliflower florets and leaves, extra chopped pistachios, and remaining 1 teaspoon sumac. Serve with flatbread.

Slow-braised lamb shoulder with beans and pomegranate molasses

PREP + COOK TIME **3 HOURS 15 MINUTES** | SERVES **4–6**

Try making your own pomegranate molasses using the recipe on page 187. This classic ingredient, used in a variety of ways in Middle Eastern cooking, imparts a sweet, tangy flavor to dishes and here works as a wonderful enhancement to the tender slow-braised lamb.

2 tbsp extra virgin olive oil, divided

1 tbsp ground cumin

1 tsp ground cinnamon

$^1/_2$ tsp ground allspice

5 lbs (2kg) bone-in lamb shoulder

$^3/_4$ cup (200g) finely chopped onion

4 garlic cloves, very thinly sliced

$^1/_4$ cup (70g) finely chopped carrot

2 cups (500ml) beef stock

$^1/_4$ cup (60ml) pomegranate molasses

1 tbsp tomato paste

$^3/_4$ cup (300g) fresh green beans, halved lengthwise

$1^1/_2$ cups (300g) couscous

$^1/_3$ cup (50g) pomegranate seeds

salt and freshly ground black pepper

1 Preheat the oven to 300°F.

2 Combine 1 tablespoon of the olive oil with the ground spices in a small bowl. Rub the spice mixture over the lamb. Season with salt and pepper to taste.

3 Heat the remaining 1 tablespoon olive oil in a large ovenproof casserole or roasting pan over high heat. Cook the lamb for 3 minutes on each side or until browned. Remove the lamb from the dish.

4 Reduce the heat to medium. Add the onion, garlic, and carrot. Cook, stirring, for 5 minutes or until softened. Add the stock, pomegranate molasses, and tomato paste. Stir to combine. Return the lamb to the casserole, including any juices.

5 Bring to a boil. Cover with a lid, then transfer to the oven. Cook for 3 hours, turning halfway through the cooking time, or until the lamb is fork tender.

6 Just before the lamb is ready, add the green beans to the casserole. Cook for 5 minutes. Transfer the lamb and beans to a large dish. Cover to keep warm. Skim any fat from the liquid in the casserole. Transfer $1^3/_4$ cups (430ml) of the mixture to a large saucepan; reserve the remainder. Bring to a boil. Add the couscous. Cover, then remove from the heat. Allow to stand for 5 minutes or until the liquid is absorbed. Fluff with a fork. Season with salt and pepper to taste.

7 Coarsely shred the lamb. Serve the lamb and beans with the couscous and remaining sauce, sprinkled with the pomegranate seeds.

Spicy white bean and meatball soup

PREP + COOK TIME **1 HOUR 55 MINUTES + OVERNIGHT SOAKING** | SERVES **4**

White bean soup, or stew, is known as "fasulye" or "fasoulia" in Turkey and across the Middle East, which translates simply as "beans." Different regions have their own variations—some with meat, some without—but its constants are the beans and the fragrant broth.

You will need to start this recipe the day before

8oz (225g) dried white beans such as haricot (see tip)

2 tbsp extra virgin olive oil, divided

½ cup (150g) finely chopped onion

½ cup (150g) finely chopped celery

⅓ cup (15g) finely chopped cilantro

2 garlic cloves, crushed

3 tsp ground coriander

2 tsp ground cinnamon

¼ tsp ground allspice

½ tsp saffron threads

1 lb (500g) ground lamb

6 cups (1.5 liters) chicken stock

¼ lb (100g) curly kale, torn

salt and freshly ground black pepper

crusty bread, to serve

TIPS

• We used haricot beans in this recipe, but other white beans such as cannellini or Great Northern are also suitable. Adjust the cooking time accordingly.

• If you like, you can swap the ground lamb for ground beef, chicken, or turkey, for something different.

1 Put the beans in a large bowl with enough water to cover. Allow to soak overnight.

2 The next day, drain the beans. Rinse under cold running water. Drain. Put the beans in a large saucepan with enough water to cover. Bring to a simmer. Cook for 30 minutes or until almost tender. Drain.

3 Meanwhile, heat 1 tablespoon of the olive oil in a large frying pan over high heat. Cook the onion, celery, and chopped cilantro, stirring, for 5 minutes or until softened. Add the garlic, ground coriander, cinnamon, and allspice. Cook for 1 minute. Remove from the heat. Allow to cool.

4 At the same time, combine the saffron and 1 tablespoon boiling water in a small cup. Allow to stand for 10 minutes to infuse.

5 Once the onion mixture has cooled, combine half of the mixture with the lamb in a large bowl. Season with salt and pepper. Roll level tablespoons of the mixture into balls.

6 Heat the remaining 1 tablespoon olive oil in a large saucepan over a medium heat. Working in 2 batches, cook the meatballs, turning, for 5 minutes or until browned. Remove from the pan. Add the saffron and its soaking liquid to the same pan with the remaining onion mixture, 2 cups (500ml) water, and the stock. Stir to combine. Add the drained beans and the meatballs. Bring to a simmer. Cook, covered, for 45 minutes until the beans are very tender. Season with salt and pepper to taste. Stir in the kale until just wilted.

7 Serve the soup with crusty bread for mopping up the broth.

Moroccan lamb, chickpea, and cilantro soup

PREP + COOK TIME **3 HOURS** | SERVES **4**

This nourishing soup, with its amalgam of meat, vegetables, grains, and pulses, combines the myriad flavors and ingredients of North African cooking in one delicious pot. A variation on harira, without the rice or noodles often added for everyday eating, it is still a meal in itself.

3¹/₂ lbs (1.7kg) bone-in lamb shoulder

2 tbsp extra virgin olive oil, divided

3¹/₂ cups (100g) fresh cilantro

¹/₂ cup (150g) finely chopped onion

¹/₂ cup (180g) sliced carrot

1 tbsp ground coriander

1 tbsp ground cumin

1 tsp ground turmeric

¹/₂ tsp dried pepper flakes

2 hot peppers, seeded, thinly sliced

6 cups (1.5 liters) beef stock

¹/₂ cup (100g) freekeh

1 15.5 oz (439g) can chickpeas, drained, rinsed

³/₄ lb (400g) vine tomatoes, quartered

salt and freshly ground black pepper

Greek yogurt and toasted Turkish pide or pita bread, to serve

1 Season the lamb with salt and pepper to taste. Heat 1 tablespoon of the olive oil in a large casserole or stockpot over high heat. Cook the lamb for 5 minutes, turning, until well browned. Remove from the dish.

2 Finely chop the cilantro, reserving leaves for serving. Heat the remaining 1 tablespoon olive oil in the same casserole. Cook the onion and carrot, stirring, for 5 minutes or until softened. Add the chopped cilantro, ground coriander, cumin, turmeric, pepper flakes, and hot peppers. Cook for a further 1 minute or until fragrant.

3 Return the lamb to the casserole with the stock. Bring to a simmer. Cook, covered, for 2 hours. Add the freekeh. Cook for 15 minutes. Add the chickpeas and tomatoes. Cook for a further 15 minutes or until the lamb is falling off the bone and the freekeh is tender. Remove the lamb. Shred the meat, discarding the bone. Skim any fat from the soup. Return the meat to pan. Season with salt and pepper to taste.

4 Ladle the soup into serving bowls, then top with the reserved cilantro. Serve with yogurt and pita bread.

Red lentil, bulgur wheat, and shrimp stew

PESCATARIAN | PREP + COOK TIME **50 MINUTES** | SERVES **4**

This stew is altogether warming from the fresh hot peppers, light from the shrimp, and hearty from the lentils. Ras el hanout adds its distinctive mark. This spice mix, considered to be a superior blend made of only the best spices, is used in Morocco, Tunisia, and Algeria.

2 tbsp extra virgin olive oil

1/2 cup (150g) finely chopped onion

1 hot pepper seeded, finely chopped, plus extra, sliced, to serve

2 garlic cloves, crushed

2 tsp ras el hanout

6 cups (1.5 liters) vegetable stock

8oz (225g) plum tomatoes, halved

1 cup (200g) dried red lentils

1/2 cup (90g) coarse bulgur wheat, well rinsed

2 lbs (900g) uncooked shrimp, peeled, deveined, tails intact

salt and freshly ground black pepper

mint sprinkle

1 cup (50g) finely chopped mint leaves

1 tbsp finely chopped preserved lemon (see page 187)

1 tsp ground sumac

1 garlic clove, crushed

1 tbsp lemon juice

1/4 lb (100g) cherry tomatoes, finely chopped

1   Heat the olive oil in a large saucepan over medium heat. Cook the onion and pepper for 3 minutes or until softened. Add the garlic and ras el hanout. Cook for 1 minute or until fragrant. Next, add the stock, tomatoes, lentils, and bulgur wheat; bring to a simmer. Cook, covered, for 15 minutes or until the lentils and bulgur wheat are just cooked. Add the shrimp. Cook, covered, for a further 5 minutes or until they are just cooked. Season with salt and pepper to taste.

2   Meanwhile, to make the mint sprinkle, combine the ingredients in a small bowl. Season with salt and pepper to taste.

3   Serve the stew topped with the mint sprinkle and extra sliced pepper.

Loads of greens stew with cumin chicken meatballs

PREP + COOK TIME **45 MINUTES** | SERVES **4**

A wholesome supper any day of the week, this contemporary twist on Middle Eastern flavors also works well as part of a banquet-style meal. The warmth of the cumin and turmeric, combined with the sweetness of dates, lifts the meatballs out of the ordinary.

¼ cup (60ml) extra virgin olive oil, divided

¼ cup (80g) thinly sliced onion

3 garlic cloves, finely chopped

1 tbsp cumin seeds

2 tsp ground turmeric

1 lb (500g) ground chicken

¼ cup (60g), chopped, pitted fresh dates such as Medjool

4 cups (1 liter) chicken stock

1 x 15.5oz (439g) can chickpeas, drained, rinsed

½ cup (100g) couscous

½ lb (240g) zucchini, thinly sliced

10oz (300g) Swiss chard, thickly sliced

5oz (150g) green beans, halved lengthwise

salt and freshly ground black pepper

warmed pita bread, to serve (optional)

lemon wedges, to serve

1 Heat 1 tablespoon of the olive oil in a large, deep nonstick saucepan over medium heat. Cook the onion and garlic, stirring often, for 5 minutes or until soft. Add the cumin and turmeric. Cook for a further minute or until fragrant. Transfer to a large bowl. Allow to cool slightly.

2 Add the ground chicken and dates to the onion mixture in the bowl; season well with salt and pepper. Mix until well combined. Using your hands, roll about 2 tablespoons each of the mixture into balls to make 12 meatballs in total.

3 Heat the remaining olive oil in the same pan over medium heat. Cook the meatballs, in batches and turning often, for 5 minutes or until golden. Carefully remove from the pan; set aside to keep warm.

4 Add the stock and chickpeas to the pan. Cook, scraping the bottom of the pan occasionally, for 12 minutes or until the liquid is slightly reduced. Return the meatballs with any juices to the pan. Simmer, covered, for 5 minutes or until almost cooked.

5 Add the couscous and vegetables. Stir gently to combine. Cook, covered, for a further 3 minutes or until the meatballs, vegetables, and couscous are just tender.

6 Serve the stew and meatballs with warmed pita bread, if you like, and lemon wedges for squeezing over.

Chicken baharat stew with yogurt and pistachios

PREP + COOK TIME **1 HOUR 20 MINUTES + STANDING** | SERVES **4**

Baharat may be an all-purpose spice mix, but its smoky warmth adds a distinctive depth and flavour to all sorts of dishes from stews and soups to meat and vegetable dishes. To take advantage of this, serve the chicken with rice to soak up all the scrumptious juices.

2 tbsp baharat

2 dried chile peppers (10g)

1 tbsp honey

2 tbsp extra virgin olive oil, divided

3½ lbs (1.4kg) chicken legs

¾ cup (200g) thinly sliced onion

4 garlic cloves, crushed

2 cups (500ml) chicken stock

1 lb (500g) cherry tomatoes

1 lb (500g) new potatoes, halved

2 wedges of preserved lemon (80g), pulp removed, zest thinly sliced (see page 187)

½ cup (15g) coarsely chopped flat-leaf parsley

¼ cup (35g) slivered pistachios

salt and freshly ground black pepper

½ cup (140g) Greek yogurt, to serve

1 Preheat the oven to 350°F.

2 Combine the baharat, chiles, honey, and 1 tablespoon of the olive oil in a large bowl. Add the chicken. Turn to coat well. Season with salt and pepper to taste.

3 Heat the remaining 1 tablespoon olive oil in a large ovenproof casserole over medium heat. Add the chicken, skin-side down, to the dish. Cook, turning, for 4 minutes or until just starting to brown. Remove from the casserole; set aside to keep warm.

4 Add the onion and garlic to the casserole with ¼ cup (60ml) water. Cook, stirring often, for 4 minutes or until the onion is soft. Add the stock, tomatoes, and chicken with any juices. Cover; transfer to the oven. Cook for 30 minutes. Add the potatoes. Return to the oven, covered, for a further 30 minutes or until the chicken and potatoes are tender. Allow to stand for 10 minutes.

5 To serve, top the stew with the preserved lemon zest, parsley, and pistachios. Season with salt to taste. Serve with the yogurt.

TIP

Use 4 chicken thighs (skin on) and 4 chicken drumsticks instead of whole chicken legs, if you like.

Lamb and lemon dukkah meatball tagine

PREP + COOK TIME **45 MINUTES** | SERVES **4**

The Egyptian condiment dukkah, made up of a blend of nuts, herbs, and spices, has gained widespread popularity outside the Middle East. Often used in Egypt as a dip served with olive oil and bread, as well as vegetables, here it gives the meatballs a powerful flavor boost.

1 lb (500g) ground lamb

1 cup (70g) fresh bread crumbs made from day-old bread

1 egg, lightly beaten

¼ cup (80g) grated onion, plus ¼ cup (80g) thinly sliced onion

2 garlic cloves

1 tsp fennel seeds

⅓ cup (35g) dukkah, plus extra, to serve (optional)

¼ cup (60ml) extra virgin olive oil, divided

1 tbsp cumin seeds

4 cups (1 liter) chicken stock

1 cup (120g) Sicilian green olives

8oz (225g) frozen garden peas

1 tbsp honey

2 lemons (280g), thinly sliced

1 cup (30g) cilantro leaves

pearl couscous, to serve

toasted flaked almonds, to serve

1 Combine the ground lamb, bread crumbs, beaten egg, grated onion, garlic, fennel seeds, and the ⅓ cup (35g) dukkah in a large bowl. Mix well. Form heaped tablespoons of the mixture into balls to make 16 meatballs in total.

2 Heat 1 tablespoon of the olive oil in a large non-stick sauté pan over medium heat. Cook the sliced onion and cumin, stirring occasionally, for 6 minutes or until soft and light golden. Transfer to a small bowl; set aside.

3 Heat the remaining olive oil in the sauté pan. Cook the meatballs for 5 minutes, turning halfway through the cooking time, or until browned. Increase the heat to medium-high. Return the onion mixture to the sauté pan with the chicken stock and olives. Cook for 20 minutes or until the stock is reduced in volume by half.

4 Add the peas and honey. Stir gently to combine, then top with the lemon slices. Cook, covered, for a further 5 minutes over medium heat or until the lemon is soft and the meatballs and peas are cooked.

5 To serve, top the tagine with the cilantro leaves and an extra sprinkling of dukkah, if you like. Serve with pearl couscous and toasted almonds.

TIPS

- You could use ground beef or turkey in this recipe, if you like.
- The lemon slices add a lovely flavor to the tagine, but it's best to remove most of them before serving because the oils in the pith can make it bitter.

Banquet menu

When it comes to choosing dishes for a banquet-style meal, you may feel spoiled for choice—but achieving balance when making your selection is not difficult at all. Simply be sure to include examples from across the book, including the mezze chapter, representing the various styles and methods of cooking used. And always remember to have the obligatory condiments, pickles, and dips on hand.

BANQUET RECIPES

1 Loads of greens stew with cumin chicken meatballs PAGE 150
2 Turkish-style braised red mullet PAGE 130
3 Lentil and sumac phyllo rolls SEE MEZZE PAGE 30
4 Kabocha squash fatteh with almond tarator
SEE VEGETABLES AND SALADS PAGE 60

DESSERTS

Redolent with the tastes and aromas of the
Middle East, these evocative sweet treats
will lure you in and satisfy your sweet
cravings in the most glorious way.

Upside-down grape, honey, and pine nut cake

PREP + COOK TIME **1 HOUR 30 MINUTES + STANDING** | SERVES **8**

Pine nuts are much prized in Middle Eastern and North African cooking in both savory and sweet dishes. A source of food in Europe and Asia for millennia, they have been an integral element of Arab and other regional cuisines since medieval times.

6 sprigs of thyme

$^1/_2$ lb (250g) seedless red grapes, halved

$^1/_2$ cup (80g) pine nuts, lightly toasted

$^1/_2$ cup (180g) honey

4 eggs

$^1/_2$ cup (125ml) extra virgin olive oil, plus extra for greasing

$^1/_3$ cup (95g) Greek yogurt

1 tsp finely grated orange zest

$1^1/_4$ cup (150g) all-purpose flour

$^2/_3$ cup (100g) whole-wheat flour

1 tsp baking soda

2 tsp baking powder

$^1/_2$ tsp salt

extra bunches of red grapes, to serve (see tips)

orange-cinnamon syrup

$^1/_3$ cup (80ml) orange juice

4 tbsp butter

1 cup (220g) firmly packed light soft brown sugar

$^1/_2$ tsp ground cinnamon

TIPS

- Due to the honey, oil, and fruit content, this cake is cooked at a lower than usual temperature to prevent overbrowning. It is best made on the day of serving.
- We used a variety of small red grapes and Champagne grapes to top the cake.

1 Preheat the oven to 275°F (see tip). Grease a 9-in round cake pan, then line with parchment paper without extending it above the edge of the pan.

2 To make the orange-cinnamon syrup, put the ingredients in a small heavy-based saucepan over medium heat. Bring to a boil, stirring, until well combined. Simmer for 3 minutes or until the syrup has thickened slightly. Pour three-quarters of the syrup into the prepared cake pan. Allow to cool for 5 minutes, reserving the remaining syrup.

3 Arrange the sprigs of thyme over the syrup in the pan. Taking care, as the syrup will be hot, scatter the grapes evenly over the bottom of the pan. Sprinkle with 2 tablespoons of the pine nuts to fill any gaps until the syrup is covered.

4 Using an electric mixer, beat together the honey and eggs in a large bowl on high speed for 8 minutes or until almost tripled in volume. Gradually add the olive oil, then the yogurt and orange zest, beating briefly until just combined.

5 Sift together both flours, the baking soda, baking powder, and salt. Gently fold the dry mixture and remaining pine nuts through the egg mixture, taking care not to deflate the mixture. Pour the mixture into the cake pan. Level the surface.

6 Bake on the lowest shelf of the oven for 1 hour 10 minutes or until a skewer inserted into the centre of the cake comes out clean. Allow to cool in the pan for 15 minutes.

7 Run a knife around the edge of the pan to loosen the parchment paper. While the pan is still hot, carefully invert the cake onto a cake plate. Remove the parchment paper. Allow to cool completely. Warm the remaining syrup and pour over the cake. Top the cake with extra grapes to serve.

Peach clafoutis with honey and rose syrup

PREP + COOK TIME **50 MINUTES** | SERVES **6**

This luscious dessert, made in the style of a French cherry clafoutis, incorporates the classic Middle Eastern ingredients of rosewater, honey, stone fruit, and nuts. A feast for the eyes as well as the taste buds, it couldn't be simpler to put together.

4 eggs, lightly beaten

2 cups (500ml) milk

³/₄ cup (115g) all-purpose flour

2 tbsp sugar

1 tsp ground cinnamon

¹/₂ tsp salt

2 tbsp (30g) butter

1³/₄ lbs (800g) large yellow peaches, pits removed, cut into wedges

2 tbsp blanched slivered pistachios (optional)

ice cream, crème fraîche, or Greek yogurt, to serve

honey and rose syrup

¹/₂ cup (175g) honey

1 vanilla pod, split lengthwise, seeds scraped (reserve pod)

1 tbsp unsprayed dried rose petals

1 tbsp rosewater

1 Preheat the oven to 425°F.

2 Whisk together the eggs and milk in a small bowl. Combine the flour, sugar, cinnamon, and salt in a large bowl. Make a well in the center. Gradually whisk in the egg mixture until smooth; do not overbeat.

3 Melt the butter in a large, ovenproof skillet. Arrange the peach wedges over the bottom of the pan. Bake for 10 minutes or until the peaches start to soften. Remove the pan from the oven. Quickly pour the batter over the fruit, then immediately return the pan to the oven. Bake for 15 minutes. Reduce the oven temperature to 350°F. Bake for a further 15 minutes or until puffed and golden.

4 Meanwhile, to make the honey and rose syrup, combine the honey, vanilla seeds and pod, rose petals, and ¹/₂ cup (125ml) water in a small saucepan over medium heat. Simmer for 15 minutes or until thickened. Stir in the rosewater. Allow to cool slightly. Discard the vanilla pod.

5 To serve, drizzle the clafoutis with the syrup and sprinkle with the pistachios, if you like. Serve with ice cream.

Pot-roasted quince with brown sugar labneh

PREP + COOK TIME **3 HOURS 40 MINUTES + 24 HOUR REFRIGERATION** | SERVES **4**

Known to some ancient civilizations as "golden apples," quinces have been cultivated since the beginnings of agriculture in the Mesopotamian plain and beyond. Sweetening the labneh with brown sugar adds a wonderfully molasses-like flavor to its tangy creaminess.

You will need to start this recipe the day before

1¹/₂ cups (330g) sugar

¹/₂ cup (175g) honey

3 fresh bay leaves

2 star anise

4 small quinces (800g), unpeeled, washed, halved (see tips)

brown sugar labneh

2 cups (500g) Greek yogurt

¹/₄ cup (55g) firmly packed light brown sugar

¹/₂ tsp ground star anise

1 To make the brown sugar labneh, place a sieve over a bowl. Line with 2 layers of cheesecloth. Combine the yogurt, sugar, and star anise in a medium bowl. Spoon the yogurt mixture into the cheese cloth. Gather the corners to form a ball; secure with string or an elastic band, and place in a strainer over a bowl. Refrigerate for 24 hours or until thickened.

2 The next day, preheat the oven to 300°F.

3 Combine the sugar, honey, 2 cups (500ml) water, bay leaves, and star anise in a medium saucepan. Bring to a boil over medium heat, stirring to dissolve the sugar. Add the quince halves to a baking dish, tucking them in to fit snugly in the dish. Cover with a tight-fitting lid.

4 Place the baking dish in the oven. Roast the quinces, turning halfway through the cooking time, for 3 hours or until tender and deep red in color. (The cooking time for the quinces will vary, depending on the ripeness and age of the fruit, and may take up to an extra hour.)

5 Transfer 1 cup (250ml) of the syrup to a small saucepan. Simmer over medium heat for 5 minutes or until reduced in volume by half.

6 Serve the quinces with the labneh and syrup.

TIPS

• Quince skin is edible, so they don't need peeling. If the skin has down on it, you can rub it away with a dish towel.

• Quinces are high in pectin and a lot of it is contained in the skin, so you may find that the cooking liquid gels like jam.

• You can also buy pre-made labneh in the dairy section of some grocery stores.

Stone fruit tahini crumble

PREP + COOK TIME **1 HOUR** | SERVES **6**

Tahini and stone fruit combine to form an unexpected culinary match made in heaven.
The nuttiness of this classic sesame paste brings out the juicy sweetness in the fruit's flesh,
while the crunchy chewiness of the crumble topping provides textural contrast.

1 lb (450g) plums, halved, pits removed

³/₄ lb (340g) nectarines, quartered, pits removed

³/₄ lb (330g) cherries, pitted

¹/₃ cup (115g) honey

2 tbsp melted butter

2 tbsp lemon juice

2 tsp orange blossom water (see tips)

tahini crumble

1 cup (90g) rolled oats

¹/₂ cup (75g) coarsely chopped pistachios

¹/₃ cup (40g) almond meal

¹/₂ tsp ground cinnamon

¹/₂ tsp ground ginger

2 tbsp extra virgin olive oil

2 tbsp honey

2 tbsp tahini

1 Preheat the oven to 350°F. Grease a 10-cup (2.5-liter) 8 x 12in baking dish.

2 Put the plums, nectarines, and cherries in the prepared dish. Combine the honey, butter, lemon juice, and orange blossom water in a bowl. Pour over the fruit. Toss to coat. Bake for 5 minutes.

3 Meanwhile, to make the tahini crumble, combine the oats, pistachios, almond meal, and spices in a medium bowl. Add the olive oil, tahini, and honey. Using your hands, rub the wet ingredients with the dry ingredients until the mixture clumps.

4 Top the fruit with the crumble mixture. Bake for 35 minutes or until the fruit is tender and the crumble is golden. Serve warm.

TIPS

- Orange blossom water is produced by distilling the fragrant nectar of spring-blooming orange blossoms. It is available at Middle Eastern grocers and many supermarkets. If unavailable, substitute with finely grated orange zest.
- This crumble is best made close to serving; however, if made ahead of time, it reheats well.

Halva ice-cream cake with coffee dates

PREP + COOK TIME **50 MINUTES + STANDING + FREEZING** | SERVES **8**

In its simplest form, sesame halva could be seen as just tahini and sugar. It's not so simple, though, and our taste buds thank us for it. The method used to add caramelized sugar to tahini creates a tender confection that crumbles and melts in your mouth.

$1/2$ gallon (2 liters) vanilla ice cream

8oz (225g) chocolate sesame halva, chopped

$1/2$ cup (70g) sesame seeds, toasted, divided

8oz (225g) fresh dates, halved, pitted

$2/3$ cup (80ml) instant espresso

$1^2/3$ cups (370g) sugar, divided

1 Allow the ice cream to stand at room temperature for 20 minutes or until slightly softened.

2 Line a 7-in round cake pan with plastic wrap.

3 Put the softened ice cream, halva, and $1/4$ cup (35g) of the sesame seeds in a large bowl. Using a large metal spoon, gently fold the mixture until just combined. Spoon into the prepared cake pan; smooth the surface. Cover the pan with plastic wrap. Freeze for 4 hours or overnight until completely firm.

4 To make the coffee dates, put the dates, espresso, $2/3$ cup (150g) of the sugar, and $2/3$ cup (160ml) water in a medium saucepan over medium heat. Simmer for 5 minutes. Allow to cool. Using a hand-held blender, blend until smooth. Transfer to a bowl; cover. Refrigerate until needed.

5 Sprinkle the remaining $1/4$ cup (35g) sesame seeds onto a large baking sheet lined with parchment paper. Put the remaining 1 cup (220g) sugar and 1 cup (250ml) water in a small saucepan over medium heat. Cook, stirring continuously, until the sugar dissolves. Simmer, without stirring, for 15 minutes or until dark golden. Quickly pour over the sesame seeds, tilting the sheet to cover. Allow to cool. Break into large shards. Store in an airtight container until needed.

6 Dip the bottom of the cake pan into a sink filled with a little hot water for a few seconds. Turn out the halva ice cream onto a large plate. Peel off the plastic wrap. If necessary, smooth the top and side with a spatula. Freeze until ready to serve.

7 Just before serving, spread the espresso-date mixture over the top of the ice-cream cake. Decorate with the sesame toffee shards and extra sesame seeds, if you like.

TIPS

• Sesame halva, halwa, or halvah is a confectionery made from sesame seeds and sugar. It is available from supermarkets, delis, and specialist grocers.

• The recipe can be made a week ahead. Store the ice-cream cake in the freezer, espresso dates in the fridge, and toffee shards in an airtight container in the fridge. Assemble when ready to serve.

Persian love cakes

PREP + COOK TIME **1 HOUR 5 MINUTES + COOLING** | MAKES **6**

We love our version of this fragrant, spiced cake with the magical name. By baking the crust briefly before adding the cake mixture, you get the best of both worlds—a crisp, nutty base and a delectable, moist top.

1/4 cup (35g) shelled pistachios, plus extra, finely chopped, to serve

1 1/2 cups (330g) turbinado or cane sugar

3 cups (360g) almond meal

1/2 tsp ground cardamom

1/4 cup (125g) butter, softened, chopped, plus extra for greasing

2 eggs

1 cup (280g) Greek yogurt

3 tsp rosewater

1/3 cup (55g) fine semolina

1/4 tsp ground nutmeg

unsprayed fresh rose petals, to serve (optional)

rosewater icing

1 cup (160g) powdered sugar, sifted

1 tsp rosewater

3 tsp lemon juice

1 Preheat the oven to 400°F. Grease six 1 1/2 cup (375ml), three 1/2-in diameter ramekins or small cake pans. Lay a narrow strip of parchment paper across the bottom of each ramekin and with the edges extended above the dish (to serve as a "handle"). Top with a parchment paper round in the bottom of each dish.

2 In a food processor, pulse the pistachios and sugar until finely ground. Add the almond meal, cardamom, and butter. Process until the mixture resembles fine bread crumbs. Reserve half of the nut mixture in a small bowl. Divide the remaining nut mixture among the lined dishes, pressing evenly over the bottom.

3 Place the dishes on a baking sheet. Bake for 10 minutes or until light golden. Remove from the oven. Allow to cool in the dishes while making the filling. Reduce the oven temperature to 350°F.

4 Return the reserved nut mixture to the food processor with the eggs, yogurt, rosewater, semolina, and nutmeg. Process until smooth. Pour the mixture onto the bases in the dishes.

5 Bake the cakes for 35 minutes or until golden and a skewer inserted into the center comes out clean. Allow the cakes to cool in the dishes for 45 minutes. Using the sling "handles," carefully lift out the cakes; transfer to a wire rack to cool completely.

6 To make the rosewater icing, whisk together the powdered sugar, rosewater, and lemon juice in a small bowl until smooth.

7 To serve, spread the cooled cakes with the rosewater icing, allowing it to run down the sides a little. Decorate with the rose petals and extra finely chopped pistachios.

TIP

The cakes will keep in an airtight container for up to 3 days.

Salted dark chocolate and tahini tart

PREP + COOK TIME **50 MINUTES + REFRIGERATION + COOLING** | SERVES **12**

Although tahini is more often used for savory dishes than sweet, when paired with sugar and chocolate, it elevates this simple sesame paste to a dessert pantry staple, taking it well out of the realm of "just for hummus."

2 eggs, plus extra 3 yolks

1/3 cup (75g) sugar

10oz (260g) dark chocolate (70% cocoa), coarsely chopped

1/2 cup plus 6 tbsp (185g) butter

1/2 cup (140g) tahini

1 tsp salt

1 cup (280g) Greek yogurt

sesame halva, crumbled, to serve

chocolate pastry

1 1/3 cups (200g) all-purpose flour

1/3 cup (55g) powdered sugar

3/4 cup (70g) Dutch-process cocoa powder (see tip)

7 tbsp (110g) cold unsalted butter, chopped

3 egg yolks

2 tbsp chilled water

1 To make the chocolate pastry, in a food processor, combine the flour, powdered sugar, and cocoa. Add the butter. Pulse until the mixture resembles fine crumbs. Add the egg yolks and chilled water. Pulse until just combined. Turn the pastry onto a lightly floured work surface. Form into a disc, then wrap in plastic wrap. Refrigerate for 1 hour.

2 Lightly oil a 9-in round, 1-in deep loose-bottomed tart pan. Roll the pastry between 2 sheets of parchment paper until large enough to line the pan. Lift the pastry into the pan, pressing into the bottom and sides. (Leave any excess pastry overhanging the side; the edge is trimmed after baking.) Cover; refrigerate for 1 hour.

3 Preheat the oven to 350°F. Place the tart pan on a baking sheet. Line the pastry with parchment paper. Fill with dried beans or pie weights. Bake for 10 minutes. Remove the paper and weights. Bake for a further 10 minutes or until the pastry is just cooked. Allow to cool in the pan; do not turn off the oven.

4 Meanwhile, whisk together the eggs, extra yolks, and sugar in a large bowl until pale. In a separate heatproof bowl, add the chocolate, butter, 1/4 cup (70g) of the tahini, and the salt in a medium heatproof bowl over a saucepan of simmering water. Stir occasionally until melted and combined. Fold the chocolate mixture into the egg mixture.

5 Using a small serrated knife, carefully trim the edge of the pastry level with the pan. Pour the chocolate filling into the tart case. Dollop the remaining 1/4 cup (70g) tahini in small spoonfuls over the filling. Using a metal skewer, gently swirl through the chocolate mixture.

6 Bake the tart for 30 minutes or until the filling is just set. Allow to cool. Serve the tart topped with the yogurt and crumbled halva.

TIP

Dutch-process cocoa powder is darker than natural cocoa powder and has a mellower flavor. It goes through an alkalizing process when it is made, neutralizing the natural acidity of the cocoa beans.

Black sesame cookie and honey ice-cream sandwiches

PREP + COOK TIME **1 HOUR + FREEZING** | MAKES **6**

Made from black sesame seeds, black tahini has a deeper, nuttier flavor than its blond counterpart. Black sesame seeds have been used in Middle Eastern desserts for centuries. These treats, a contemporary twist on this, are mouthwateringly tempting.

1½ cups (180g) almond meal

½ tsp baking soda

½ tsp salt

⅓ cup (90g) black tahini

⅓ cup (115g) honey

1 tsp vanilla bean paste

¼ cup (50g) black sesame seeds

honey ice cream

1 cup (350g) honey

⅓ cup (75g) sugar

1½ cups (420g) Greek yogurt

1½ cups (375ml) heavy cream

¼ cup (60ml) lemon juice

1 To make the honey ice cream, stir the honey and sugar in a small saucepan over medium heat until the sugar is dissolved. Allow to cool. Combine the yogurt, cream, and lemon juice in a large bowl. Stir in the cooled honey syrup. Pour the mixture into a freezer-proof container. Cover. Freeze for 2-3 hours or refrigerate overnight. Pour the mixture in the food processor and process in two batches until smooth. Refreeze in a 9 x 9-in baking dish covered with plastic wrap. Freeze for 6 hours or overnight.

2 Preheat the oven to 325°F. Line a large baking sheet with parchment paper.

3 Combine the almond meal, baking soda, and salt in a large bowl. Add the tahini, honey, and vanilla bean paste. Stir until well combined. Roll heaped tablespoons of the mixture into balls. You will make 12. Put the sesame seeds in a small bowl. Toss the balls in the seeds, pressing to coat. Place on the lined baking sheet. Using the bottom of a glass, gently flatten to make 3-in rounds.

4 Bake the cookies for 15 minutes or until firm and lightly browned. Allow to cool on the sheet for 10 minutes, before transferring to a wire rack to cool completely. The cookies will firm on cooling.

5 To assemble, use a 3-in cookie cutter to cut six rounds from the ice cream. Sandwich the rounds between the cookies. Return to the freezer until ready to serve.

TIPS

- If you have an ice-cream machine, churn the honey ice cream following the manufacturer's instructions.
- Store any leftover ice cream in the freezer for up to 1 month.
- If you prefer, you can set the ice cream in a loaf pan and scoop it rather than cut out with a cookie cutter.

Saffron labneh with pistachio phyllo fingers and honeyed apricots

PREP + COOK TIME **45 MINUTES + 24 HOUR REFRIGERATION** | SERVES **6**

An indispensable ingredient in many Middle Eastern sweets, orange blossom water brings a distinctive floral flavor with citrus overtones to dishes when it is used. It is important not to overdo it, though, as it is very strong and can easily overpower other, more delicate flavors.

You will need to start this recipe the day before

8oz (225g) shelled pistachios

¹/₂ cup (110g) sugar

1 tbsp orange blossom water

1 cup (250g) butter, divided

6 sheets of phyllo pastry (90g), thawed if frozen

2 tbsp honey

10oz (300g) apricots, halved, pits removed stones removed

saffron labneh

¹/₄ tsp saffron threads

3 cups (750g) Greek yogurt

1¹/₂ tbsp honey

¹/₂ cup (65g) finely chopped pistachios

TIPS

• While you are working, keep the remaining phyllo sheets covered with parchment paper, topped with a clean, damp dish towel, to prevent them drying out.

• You can buy labneh in the dairy case of your local natural foods store, if you'd prefer.

1 To make the saffron labneh, put the saffron and 2 teaspoons of boiling water in a small bowl. Allow to stand for 10 minutes. Place a sieve over a large bowl. Line with 2 layers of cheesecloth. Combine the yogurt, honey, and saffron mixture in a medium bowl. Spoon the mixture into the cheesecloth. Gather the corners to form a ball; secure with string or an elastic band. Refrigerate over a bowl for 24 hours or until thickened. Put the pistachios on a tray. Roll level tablespoons of the labneh mixture into 12 balls. Roll the balls in the nuts to coat. Refrigerate until needed.

2 Preheat the oven to 400°F. Line a large baking sheet with parchment paper. Pulse the pistachios in a food processor until finely chopped. Transfer to a medium bowl. Stir in the sugar and orange blossom water to combine.

3 Melt half of the butter. Place a sheet of phyllo on a clean work surface (see tips). Brush half of the sheet with melted butter, then fold in half crosswise. Brush half of the folded sheet with more butter and fold again in half crosswise. Cut the folded layers in half crosswise. Place 2 level tablespoons of pistachio mixture at one short end of each pastry stack. Brush the edge with butter. Roll to enclose the filling, tucking in the sides as you go. Place, seam-side down, on the lined sheet. Brush with butter. Repeat with pastry, melted butter, and filling to make 12 in total.

4 Bake the phyllo fingers for 15 minutes or until golden brown.

5 Meanwhile, melt the remaining butter and the honey in a large nonstick frying pan over medium heat. Swirl to combine. Add the apricots. Cook, gently stirring occasionally, for 3 minutes or until slightly softened and the sauce is syrupy.

6 Serve the phyllo fingers with the saffron labneh, apricots, and syrup.

Cardamom and citrus cheesecake

PREP + COOK TIME **2 HOURS + COOLING + REFRIGERATION** | SERVES **8**

The natural citrus notes found in cardamom complement and enhance the flavor of citrus fruits—and this baked cheesecake is a citrus extravaganza. It has a crisp base with a ginger zing, to add to the layers of flavor, and tastes exactly as good as it looks.

1 lb oranges (480g)

³/₄ lb (350g) ruby red grapefruit

2¹/₂ cups (600ml) whipping cream

8oz (226g) cream cheese, softened

4 eggs

¹/₂ cup (110g) light brown sugar, plus extra ¹/₂ cup (110g)

¹/₂ tsp ground cardamom

2 tsp green cardamom pods, bruised

1 cinnamon stick

³/₄ cup (180ml) blood orange juice

1 cup (280g) labneh

unsprayed fresh rose petals, to serve (optional)

spiced cookie base

8oz (225g) gingersnaps

¹/₄ cup (40g) flour

4 tbsp (60g) butter, chopped, plus extra for greasing

¹/₃ cup (75g) soft fresh dates such as Medjool, pitted, chopped

¹/₃ tsp salt

1 Preheat the oven to 350°F. Grease a 6 x 9-in baking pan and line the bottom and sides with parchment paper.

2 To make the spiced cookie base, pulse the ingredients in a food processor until coarse, crumbly, and the mixture comes together when pressed with your fingers. Press evenly and firmly into the bottom of the lined pan. Bake for 15 minutes or until slightly risen and golden. Let cool in the pan. Reduce the oven temperature to 300°F.

3 Meanwhile, finely grate the zest from the oranges. Cut the top and bottom off each orange. Remove the white pith by following the curve of the fruit. Cut off the zest and white pith from the grapefruit. Cut the oranges and grapefruit into cross section slices. Refrigerate until ready to serve.

4 In a food processor or with an electric mixer, combine the grated orange zest, cream, cream cheese, eggs, sugar, and ground cardamom. Mix for 1 minute or until completely smooth.

5 Pour the cheesecake filling over the cooled base. Place the pan on a baking sheet. Bake for 1 hour or until puffed and golden at the edges and just set. Allow to cool at room temperature for 1 hour. Refrigerate to cool completely.

6 Put the extra brown sugar, bruised cardamom pods, cinnamon, blood orange juice, and 2 tablespoons water in a small heavy-based saucepan. Stir over medium heat until the sugar is dissolved. Simmer for 15 minutes or until the syrup has reduced by half. Allow to cool, then strain.

7 To serve, transfer the cheesecake to a platter. Top with spoonfuls of the labneh and sliced citrus fruit, then drizzle with the blood orange syrup. Sprinkle with rose petals, if you like.

TIP

If blood orange juice is not available, use regular orange juice instead.

Spiced coffee cakes with dates

PREP + COOK TIME **1 HOUR + STANDING** | MAKES **8**

Enjoy these little cakes for breakfast or a snack. The addition of coffee is a wonderful pick-me-up, and its rich undertones are echoed in the moist, sweet dates served as an accompaniment to the spice-and-nut-filled cakes.

2/3 cup (110g) almonds

2/3 cup (100g) spelt flour

2 eggs

1/2 cup (100g) sugar

1/4 cup (90g) honey

1 tsp cinnamon

1/2 tsp allspice

1/2 tsp nutmeg

2 tbsp extra virgin olive oil

2 tbsp espresso

1 tsp baking powder

1/2 tsp baking soda

1/2 tsp salt

1/4 cup (30g) chopped walnuts

1 tbsp sesame seeds

coffee dates

1/2 cup (110g) light brown sugar

1/4 cup (60ml) espresso

8oz (225g) soft fresh dates such as Medjool, halved, seeded

1 Preheat the oven to 350°F. Grease an 8-hole (1/2-cup/125ml) mini loaf pan.

2 Process the almonds and 2 teaspoons of the flour until finely ground.

3 Using an electric mixer, beat together the eggs, sugar, honey, cinnamon, allspice, and nutmeg on medium-high speed for 10 minutes or until thick and pale. Reduce the speed to low; gradually beat in the olive oil and coffee until just combined. Stir in the nut mixture, then the sifted remaining flour, baking powder, baking soda, and salt. Spoon the mixture into the holes of the prepared pan. Sprinkle with the walnuts and sesame seeds.

4 Bake the cakes for 25 minutes. Loosen the sides of each cake with a knife. Turn each cake out of the pan and let cool on a wire rack.

5 Meanwhile, to make the coffee dates, combine the brown sugar and 1/3 cup (80ml) water in a medium saucepan over medium heat. Bring to a boil, stirring to dissolve the sugar. Simmer for 2 minutes. Stir in the coffee. Return to a boil. Add the dates, remove from the heat, and set aside to cool.

6 Serve the cakes warm, with the coffee dates spooned over the top.

TIPS

- These cakes are best made on day of serving, but can be frozen, tightly wrapped in plastic wrap, for up to 2 months. The coffee dates can be made 2 days ahead. Store, covered, in the fridge until needed.
- If you don't have spelt flour, you can use whole wheat flour instead.

Pure apple and cardamom cake

PREP + COOK TIME **3 HOURS + COOLING, REFRIGERATION + STANDING** | SERVES **8**

As this tempting "cake" is made entirely of apples, it is a gluten-free-friendly option for people who cannot eat gluten. You can serve this dessert with custard, softly whipped cream, or even ice cream, for something different, instead or in addition to the mascarpone cheese.

1 vanilla pod, split lengthwise, seeds scraped out (reserve pod)

1 cinnamon stick

$^2/_3$ cup (150g) sugar

$^1/_2$ cup (125ml) apple juice (see tip)

2 tbsp lemon juice

6 tbsp (80g) butter, chopped, plus extra, to grease

4 lbs (2kg) large green apples such as Granny Smith or Golden Delicious

1 tsp honey

1 tsp maple syrup

8oz (225g) mascarpone cheese

1 Preheat the oven to 350°F. Grease 9-in springform pan and line the bottom with parchment paper.

2 Put the vanilla seeds and pod in a medium saucepan with the cinnamon, sugar, apple and lemon juices, and butter. Stir over medium heat until the sugar dissolves. Bring to a boil. Reduce the heat; simmer for 5 minutes until reduced slightly. Transfer to a large bowl.

3 Reserve 3 apples for the top layer. Working with 2 apples at a time, peel and core each apple, then cut into $^3/_8$-in slices. Put the slices in the bowl with the syrup. Toss to coat (to prevent discoloration). Drain the slices, and lay out in the springform pan, overlapping each slice by half. Cover the center with smaller slices to create a tight fit. Press firmly on the apples twice during layering, pouring any excess liquid back into the saucepan.

4 Peel the remaining 3 apples, leaving the stems intact. Using a mandoline, slice the apples horizontally through the core. Remove the seeds. Coat the slices lightly in the remaining syrup. Arrange overlapping slices in the pan. Cover with a parchment paper round, then with aluminum foil.

5 Bake for 1 hour. Remove foil and parchment paper. Reduce the oven temperature to 275°F. Bake for a further hour or until the apple is soft and a knife can easily be inserted into the layers, brushing occasionally with some of the remaining cooking liquid. Cool to room temperature.

6 Cover the pan with plastic wrap. Refrigerate for 4 hours or until cold and firm.

7 Collar from the springform pan and remove. Carefully transfer the cake from the base of the pan onto a serving plate. Allow to stand at room temperature for 1 hour. Brush the top of the apple cake with the warmed honey and maple syrup. Serve with the mascarpone cheese.

TIPS

- The cake is best made a day ahead to allow it to chill and firm.
- Use fresh apple juice from the refrigerated section of the supermarket.
- Use a mandoline or V-slicer to cut the apples. If you don't have either of these, use a sharp knife instead, taking care to slice thinly and evenly.

Rose-scented strawberries with labneh and almonds

PREP + COOK TIME **35 MINUTES + REFRIGERATION** | SERVES **4**

Distilled from crushed rose petals, rosewater imparts an incredible floral flavor to a variety of desserts and confectionery such as Turkish delight and baklava, as well as being used to flavor drinks. This is especially so in Persian cuisine, where its culinary origins lie.

You will need to start this recipe the day before

3 cups (750g) Greek yogurt

3 tsp vanilla bean paste

1/2 tsp saffron threads

1/2 tsp finely grated orange zest

1/4 cup (55g) sugar

1 tsp rosewater (or to taste)

1 lb (450g) strawberries, hulled, sliced

4oz (120g) raspberries

1/4 cup (35g) flaked almonds, toasted

1 To make the labneh, combine the yogurt, 2 teaspoons of the vanilla bean paste, saffron, and orange zest in a medium bowl. Put the yogurt mixture in a medium sieve lined with cheesecloth; set over a large bowl. Gather the ends of the cloth and tie tightly with string or a rubber band to allow the liquid to drain. Place over a bowl and refrigerate for 24 hours.

2 The next day, to make the rosewater syrup, combine the sugar, remaining 1 teaspoon vanilla bean paste, and 1/3 cup (80ml) water in a small saucepan over medium heat. Stir to dissolve the sugar. Bring to a boil; reduce the heat and simmer for 1 minute. Stir in the rosewater. Refrigerate to chill.

3 Combine the rosewater syrup, strawberries, and raspberries in a large bowl. Toss gently to combine. Spread the labneh mixture onto a serving platter; top with the strawberry-raspberry mixture. Sprinkle with the toasted almonds to serve.

TIPS

• Rosewater is a powerful ingredient. When using it, add a little at a time and taste as you go, until you arrive at a strength that suits you.

• You can buy labneh already made in the dairy case of many grocery stores.

• The saffron labneh can be made up to 5 days ahead, while the rosewater syrup can be made 2 days ahead. Store, covered, in the fridge.

Essential condiments

Across the Middle East and North Africa, condiments appear on the table as fundamental elements of any meal. While the examples here are drawn from several specific regions and cultures, all are characteristic of the approach to Middle Eastern cooking as a whole.

Zhoug

A fresh, hot, and zesty sauce from Yemen, zhoug packs a punch when served with grilled or roasted meat, seafood, and vegetables.

PREP + COOK TIME **10 MINUTES** | MAKES **2 CUPS**

In a small skillet over medium heat, toast 2 teaspoons caraway seeds, 1 teaspoon cumin seeds, $1/2$ teaspoon coriander seeds, and the seeds from 6 green cardamom pods for 2 minutes or until toasted and fragrant. Coarsely crush the seeds using a pestle or spice grinder. Combine the crushed seeds, 1 cup (50g) coarsely chopped cilantro, $1/2$ cup (15g) coarsely chopped flat-leaf parsley, 6 seeded and finely chopped long green chillies, 4 crushed garlic cloves, $1/3$ cup (80ml) lemon juice and $1/2$ cup (125ml) extra virgin olive oil in a small bowl.

Chermoula

This spice marinade from the Maghreb region of North Africa contains the core ingredients of garlic, cumin, fresh cilantro, oil, and salt. Traditionally used to flavor fish or seafood, it makes a delicious accompaniment to a variety of other dishes.

PREP + COOK TIME **30 MINUTES** | MAKES **ABOUT $3/4$ CUP (180ML)**

Blend or process $1/4$ cup (50g) coarsely chopped red onion, 1 peeled garlic clove, 1 cup (30g) cilantro leaves, 1 cup (20g) flat-leaf parsley leaves, 1 teaspoon ground cumin, 1 teaspoon smoked paprika, 1 tablespoon lemon juice, and 1 tablespoon extra virgin olive oil until almost smooth. Season with salt and freshly ground black pepper to taste. Thin the chermoula with a little more lemon juice or oil, if you like. Store in the fridge for up to 2 weeks.

Muhammara

Originally from Syria, muhammara can be served as a dip as part of a mezze, with pita bread or toasted Turkish pide bread, or as an accompaniment to grilled or roasted meat, seafood, or vegetables.

PREP + COOK TIME **10 MINUTES** | MAKES **$1^1/4$ CUPS**

Process $3/4$ cup (180g) roasted red bell peppers, 1 tablespoon extra virgin olive oil, $1/2$ cup (50g) walnuts, 1 tablespoon pomegranate molasses, and 1 tablespoon lemon juice until almost smooth. Season with salt and freshly ground black pepper to taste.

Harissa

This fiery Tunisian chile paste, sometimes made with rose petals, is also found in other parts of the Maghreb. It can be served with grilled meat, fish, and vegetables, or used as a marinade. Stir a little into Greek yogurt or mayonnaise for a spicy dipping sauce.

PREP + COOK TIME **30 MINUTES** | MAKES **ABOUT 1 CUP (250ML)**

Preheat the grill to a high heat. Quarter 1 red bell pepper; discard the seeds and any membrane. Place, skin-side up, on a lightly oiled baking sheet. Cook under the hot grill for 10 minutes or until the skin blisters and blackens. Put in a zip-top bag and let stand for 10 minutes. When steamed, peel and discard skin. Toast 1 tablespoon ground cumin and 2 teaspoons ground coriander until fragrant. Process the pepper, spices, 10 small red bird's-eye chiles with stalks removed, 5 quartered garlic cloves, 3 tbsp cilantro, and 1 teaspoon salt until smooth. Add 1 tablespoon extra virgin olive oil. Process until very smooth. Spoon into sterilized jars; seal tightly. Store in the fridge for up to 1 month.

Pomegranate molasses

Although readily available from supermarkets and Middle Eastern grocers, pomegranate molasses is not difficult to make from scratch. This syrup has a complex sweet–sour flavor and can be used in sauces, salad dressings, marinades, and some desserts. Keep an eye on it toward the end of the cooking time; you will need to reduce the heat to maintain a gentle simmer as it reduces.

PREP + COOK TIME **2¼ HOURS** | MAKES **1 CUP (250ML)**

Cut 8 large pomegranates in half. Squeeze the juice using a citrus juicer. You will need 4 cups (1 liter) of juice. Strain into a large saucepan with ½ cup (125ml) lemon juice and ½ cup (110g) sugar. Stir over low heat, without boiling, until the sugar dissolves. Bring to a boil; reduce the heat. Simmer gently, uncovered, for about 2 hours until the liquid is reduced to about 1 cup (250ml) and is thick and syrupy. Pour into a hot sterilized jar. Store in the fridge for up to 1 month.

TIP If you are lucky enough to have an abundant supply of pomegranates, this recipe is a great way to use up excess fruit.

Grandma's pink pickled turnips

Adding beets to the pickling liquid is a Middle Eastern method of coloring the turnips a rosy hue. You can eat the beets once pickled, remove them and discard. Pickles are an indispensable addition to Middle Eastern, especially Lebanese, banquets.

PREP + COOK TIME **15 MINUTES + STANDING** | MAKES **1 LITRE (4 CUPS)**

Trim 1 lb (450g) turnips and 2 oz (50g) baby beets. Cut the turnips into ½-in thick batons; slice the beets. Put the turnips in a 4-cup (1-liter) sterilized preserving jar. Top with the beets, pressing down gently to fit. Stir 2 cups (500ml) water and 4 tbsp kosher salt in a small bowl until the salt has dissolved. Pour over the vegetables, ensuring that they are completely submerged. Store in a cool, dark place for 2 days. Transfer to the fridge for 2 weeks or until the pickles are tender-crisp. Store in the fridge for up to 3 months.

Spicy marinated olives

Marinated olives add the perfect salty, spicy flavor to a mezze board or as an accompaniment to cheeses, labneh, or dips.

PREP + COOK TIME **10 MINUTES + REFRIGERATION** | MAKES **2½ CUPS**

Using a zester, remove the zest of 1 orange in long, thin strips. Add the strips of zest to a large bowl with 2 cups (350g) large green olives, 2 teaspoons toasted cumin seeds, 2 teaspoons lightly crushed toasted coriander seeds, ½ teaspoon harissa paste, 2 crushed garlic cloves, 4 sprigs of thyme, 2 fresh bay leaves, and ⅓ cup (80ml) olive oil. Toss gently to combine. Store in a sealed container in the fridge, stirring occasionally, for up to 4 weeks.

Preserved lemons

The salty tang of preserved lemon zest is an indispensable ingredient in North African cooking. It adds a real zing to any savory dish where fresh lemon is also used.

PREP + COOK TIME **15 MINUTES + STANDING** | MAKES **16 PIECES**

Halve 8 lemons lengthwise. Carefully cut each lemon in half again, without cutting all the way through. Open out the lemon halves slightly. Squeeze the lemons over a large nonreactive bowl to catch the juice; reserve the juice. Put the lemon halves in a separate non-reactive bowl with 1½ cups (450g) kosher salt, 5 fresh bay leaves, 1 teaspoon coriander seeds, and 1 teaspoon caraway seeds; mix well. Pack the lemon mixture into a 6-cup (1.5-liter) sterilized jar. Pour enough of the lemon juice—about 1 cup (250ml)—into the jar to cover the lemons. Top off with water if necessary to completely cover the lemons. Seal the jar. Label and date. Store the preserved lemons in a cool, dark place for at least 3 weeks before using. Refrigerate after opening.

TIPS To use, remove and discard the pulp. Squeeze any juice from the zest, rinse the zest well under cold running water, then slice according to the recipe. Cinnamon sticks or chiles can be added to the mixture at the same time as the bay leaves and seeds.

Conversion chart

A note on Australian measures

- One Australian metric measuring cup holds approximately 250ml.

- One Australian metric tablespoon holds 20ml.

- One Australian metric teaspoon holds 5ml.

- The difference between one country's measuring cups and another's is within a two- or three-teaspoon variance, and should not affect your cooking results.

- North America, New Zealand, and the United Kingdom use a 15ml tablespoon.

Using measures in this book

- All cup and spoon measurements are level.

- The most accurate way of measuring dry ingredients is to weigh them.

- When measuring liquids, use a clear glass or plastic jug with metric markings.

- We use large eggs with an average weight of 60g. Fruit and vegetables are assumed to be medium unless otherwise stated.

Dry measures

imperial	metric
$\frac{1}{2}$oz	15g
1oz	30g
2oz	60g
3oz	90g
4oz ($\frac{1}{4}$lb)	125g
5oz	155g
6oz	185g
7oz	220g
8oz ($\frac{1}{2}$lb)	250g
9oz	280g
10oz	315g
11oz	345g
12oz ($\frac{3}{4}$lb)	375g
13oz	410g
14oz	440g
15oz	470g
16oz (1lb)	500g
24oz (1$\frac{1}{2}$lb)	750g
32oz (2lb)	1kg

Liquid measures

imperial	metric
1 fluid oz	30ml
2 fluid oz	60ml
3 fluid oz	100ml
4 fluid oz	125ml
5 fluid oz	150ml
6 fluid oz	190ml
8 fluid oz	250ml
10 fluid oz	300ml
16 fluid oz	500ml
20 fluid oz	600ml
1$\frac{3}{4}$ pints	1000ml (1 liter)

Length measures

imperial	metric
$\frac{1}{8}$in	3mm
$\frac{1}{4}$in	6mm
$\frac{1}{2}$in	1cm
$\frac{3}{4}$in	2cm
1in	2.5cm
2in	5cm
2$\frac{1}{2}$in	6cm
3in	8cm
4in	10cm
5in	13cm
6in	15cm
7in	18cm
8in	20cm
9in	22cm
10in	25cm
11in	28cm
12in (1ft)	30cm

Oven temperatures

The oven temperatures in this book are for conventional ovens; if you have a fan-forced oven, decrease the temperature by 10–20 degrees.

	°F (Fahrenheit)	°C (Celsius)
Very slow	250	120
Slow	300	150
Moderately slow	325	160
Moderate	350	180
Moderately hot	400	200
Hot	425	220
Very hot	475	240

Index

Acknowledgments

DK would like to thank Sophia Young, Joe Reville, Amanda Chebatte, and Georgia Moore for their assistance in making this book.

The Australian Women's Weekly Test Kitchen in Sydney has developed, tested, and photographed the recipes in this book.